Arab Migration Into Europe: A Political and Social Wake-Up Call for Politicians

Arab Migration Into Europe: A Political and Social Wake-Call for Politicians

Copyright Page

TITLE: Arab Migration Into Europe: A Political and Social Wake-Call for Politicians

1ST Edition

Copyright @ 2023

Roberto M. Rodriguez. All rights reserved.

ISBN: 9798223521273

Arab Migration Into Europe: A Political and Social Wake-Up Call for Politicians

By Roberto Miguel Rodriguez

The recent mass migration of Arabs into Europe and Their Potential Political and Social Consequences

Understanding the Arab migration crisis

In recent years, Europe has experienced a significant influx of Arab migrants, leading to a complex and multifaceted crisis with potential political and social consequences. This section aims to provide politicians with a comprehensive understanding of the Arab migration crisis and its various dimensions, urging them to address the issue proactively.

The first aspect to explore is the economic impact of the mass migration. This includes analyzing the effects on local job markets, wages, and overall economic growth. By understanding these consequences, policymakers can develop strategies to mitigate any negative impacts and harness the potential benefits brought by the migrants.

Integration challenges faced by Arab migrants in European societies pose another important issue. Language barriers, discrimination, and identity formation are just a few of the hurdles these individuals encounter. Policymakers must be aware of these challenges and implement effective social and cultural integration policies to foster inclusivity and equal opportunities for all.

Security concerns also arise from the mass migration, as there is a potential risk of radicalization and terrorism. Policymakers need to carefully analyze the strain on European security systems and develop strategies to address the issue effectively, ensuring the safety and well-being of both the migrants and the host communities.

The management of the refugee crisis itself has significant political and social consequences. By examining the impact on domestic politics, public opinion, and policy-making, politicians can make informed decisions to better manage the crisis and mitigate any negative repercussions.

The influx of Arab migrants into European societies also affects social cohesion and multiculturalism. Policymakers must anticipate potential cultural clashes and tensions while promoting social integration policies that foster understanding, respect, and harmony among diverse communities.

Another consequence of the migration crisis is the rise of far-right political movements and parties. It is crucial to study their platforms, rhetoric, and impact on European politics to understand the broader political landscape and address any resulting polarization effectively.

The humanitarian response and international cooperation are vital in managing the migration crisis. By analyzing the political and social consequences of the international community's response, policymakers can identify areas for improvement and strengthen cooperation between European countries and international organizations.

The strain on healthcare and welfare systems also requires careful consideration. Policymakers must investigate the implications for healthcare access, social services, and public expenditure to ensure that these systems can adequately support both the migrants and the host populations.

Education and youth integration are key aspects of successful integration. Policymakers must explore the challenges and opportunities related to the integration of Arab migrant youth into European education systems, including language support and policies that promote social mobility.

Lastly, media representation and public perception play a crucial role in shaping the narrative surrounding the Arab migration crisis. Understanding how the issue is portrayed in the media and the impact of media on public perception and stereotypes is essential for politicians to counter any misinformation or bias and foster a more informed and empathetic public discourse.

In conclusion, this section provides politicians with a comprehensive understanding of the Arab migration crisis and its potential political and social consequences. By delving into various aspects such as economic impact, integration challenges, security concerns, refugee crisis management, and media representation, policymakers can make informed decisions and implement effective strategies to address the crisis and ensure a harmonious and inclusive Europe for all.

The push factors: reasons behind the mass migration

In this section, we will delve into the push factors that have led to the recent mass migration of Arabs into Europe. Understanding these reasons is crucial for policymakers as they assess the potential political and social consequences of this influx.

The Arab migration into Europe has been driven by a multitude of factors. Firstly, political instability and conflict in the Arab world have forced many individuals and families to seek refuge in safer countries. The ongoing conflicts in Syria, Yemen, and Libya, for example, have created a sense of insecurity and fear, prompting people to flee their homes in search of safety and stability.

Economic factors also play a significant role in this migration. High unemployment rates, lack of job opportunities, and economic downturns in Arab countries have pushed many individuals to seek better economic prospects in Europe. They hope to provide a better future for themselves and their families, escaping poverty and limited opportunities.

Additionally, social and cultural factors contribute to the migration. Discrimination, social exclusion, and limited freedoms faced by certain groups in Arab societies have propelled individuals to seek more inclusive and tolerant societies in Europe. They are searching for societies that respect individual rights, offer equal opportunities, and guarantee freedom of expression.

Moreover, the Arab migration into Europe is also influenced by aspirations for a better education and healthcare. Many individuals hope to benefit from the high-quality education systems and advanced healthcare facilities available in European countries. They see this as an opportunity to improve their own wellbeing and that of their children.

Understanding these push factors is crucial for politicians as they grapple with the consequences of mass migration. By comprehending the motivations behind this movement, policymakers can develop effective strategies to address the challenges and seize the opportunities presented by the Arab migration into Europe.

In the following sections, we will explore the potential political and social consequences of this mass migration, including the economic impact, integration challenges, security concerns, refugee crisis management, social cohesion, political polarization, humanitarian response, healthcare and welfare systems, education and youth integration, and media representation. By examining these various dimensions, we aim to provide policymakers with a comprehensive understanding of the Arab migration into Europe and its potential implications for European societies.

The pull factors: why Europe is an attractive destination

Europe has long been seen as a land of opportunity, and it is no surprise that it has become a magnet for migrants from the Arab world. While the recent mass migration of Arabs into Europe has generated heated debates and raised concerns among politicians and the general public, it is important to understand the factors that make Europe an attractive destination for these individuals.

One of the key pull factors is the potential for a better life. Many Arab migrants come from countries plagued by political instability, economic hardship, and conflict. They see Europe as a place where they can escape these challenges and build a brighter future for themselves and their families. The promise of economic prosperity, political stability, and access to a strong welfare system are all compelling reasons for Arab migrants to seek refuge in Europe.

Furthermore, the cultural and social freedoms enjoyed in Europe are also appealing to Arab migrants. Europe is known for its liberal values, respect for human rights, and multiculturalism. Arab migrants are drawn to the idea of living in a society that embraces diversity and offers greater personal freedom. They see Europe as a place where they can practice their religion, express their opinions, and live without fear of persecution.

Education is another significant pull factor for Arab migrants. European countries are known for their high-quality education systems, which offer opportunities for personal and professional development. Arab migrants recognize the value of education in securing a better future for themselves and their children. They see Europe as a place where they can access quality education and gain the skills needed to succeed in a globalized world.

Lastly, the perception of Europe as a safe haven is a powerful pull factor for Arab migrants. Many of them have witnessed violence and experienced trauma in their home countries. Europe is seen as a place of relative peace and security, where they can rebuild their lives in a safe environment.

However, it is important to note that while Europe may be an attractive destination, the journey itself is often perilous and fraught with risks. Arab migrants face numerous challenges, including language barriers, discrimination, and the need to navigate complex asylum systems. It is crucial for policymakers to address these challenges and develop comprehensive integration policies to ensure the successful integration of Arab migrants into European societies.

In conclusion, Europe's pull factors, including economic opportunities, cultural and social freedoms, access to quality education, and the perception of safety, make it an attractive destination for Arab migrants. However, it is essential for politicians to recognize the challenges faced by these individuals and develop effective policies to ensure their successful integration and to address the potential political and social consequences of the mass migration.

The scale of the migration: numbers and trends

In recent years, Europe has witnessed an unprecedented influx of Arab migrants, creating a significant demographic shift and posing numerous challenges for policymakers. Understanding the scale of this migration is crucial in order to effectively address the political, social, and economic consequences that accompany it.

The numbers are staggering. According to the United Nations High Commissioner for Refugees (UNHCR), over one million Arab migrants arrived in Europe in 2015 alone. This influx has continued, albeit at a slightly lower rate, in subsequent years. These numbers highlight the urgency of the issue and the need for comprehensive policies and strategies to manage the integration process.

Examining the trends within this migration is equally important. It is crucial to understand the factors that push migrants to leave their home countries and the pull factors that attract them to Europe. Economic instability, political unrest, and armed conflicts in Arab countries have been major push factors. The desire for safety, security, and better economic opportunities are among the main pull factors. By understanding these trends, policymakers can develop targeted solutions that address the specific needs of Arab migrants.

The scale and trends of this migration have profound implications across various domains. Economically, the mass migration of Arabs into Europe can impact local job markets, wages, and overall economic growth. Policymakers must carefully consider the potential consequences and develop strategies to mitigate any negative effects, such as unemployment or wage suppression, while harnessing the potential benefits of a diverse workforce.

Additionally, the integration challenges faced by Arab migrants in European societies are significant. Language barriers, discrimination, and identity formation are just a few of the obstacles that need to be addressed. Policymakers must prioritize social and cultural integration to ensure the successful inclusion of Arab migrants into European societies, promoting a sense of belonging and social cohesion.

Furthermore, security concerns cannot be ignored. The potential risk of radicalization, terrorism, and the strain on European security systems require careful attention. Policymakers need to strike a delicate balance between maintaining security and upholding fundamental human rights.

In conclusion, understanding the scale and trends of the migration of Arabs into Europe is essential for policymakers. By examining the numbers, analyzing the push and pull factors, and considering the implications across various domains such as the economy, integration, security, and social cohesion, effective policies can be developed. This section aims to provide politicians with the necessary knowledge to make informed decisions and address the challenges posed by this migration crisis.

The political and social consequences of mass migration

The political and social consequences of mass migration have become a pressing issue in recent years, particularly with the influx of Arab migrants into Europe. This section aims to provide a comprehensive analysis of these consequences, addressing the concerns and interests of politicians and the niches of the recent mass migration of Arabs into Europe and their potential political and social consequences.

One key aspect to consider is the economic impact of this mass migration. The book explores the effects on local job markets, wages, and economic growth. It delves into the potential benefits and challenges that arise, including the potential strain on social services and the need for economic integration policies.

Integration challenges are also a critical aspect to examine. The section delves into the social and cultural integration challenges faced by Arab migrants in European societies, such as language barriers, discrimination, and identity formation. It highlights the need for inclusive policies that promote social cohesion and support the successful integration of migrants.

Security concerns are another crucial aspect that requires attention. The section analyzes the potential security implications, including the risk of radicalization, terrorism, and the strain on European security systems. It offers insights into the importance of effective border control, intelligence sharing, and counter-terrorism measures.

The refugee crisis management is a significant political and social consequence that needs exploration. The book investigates the impact on domestic politics, public opinion, and policy-making. It emphasizes the need for effective and humane management of the crisis, while also addressing the concerns of the host communities.

Social cohesion and multiculturalism are also key themes discussed. The section examines the effects of Arab migration on social cohesion and multiculturalism in European societies, including potential cultural clashes, tensions, and the need for social integration policies. It emphasizes the importance of fostering understanding, respect, and dialogue among diverse communities.

The rise of far-right political movements and parties in response to the mass migration is another critical aspect to study. The book delves into the platforms, rhetoric, and impact of these movements on European politics. It explores strategies to counteract polarization and promote inclusive political discourse.

Humanitarian response and international cooperation are also crucial components of the analysis. The section analyzes the political and social consequences of the international community's response to the migration crisis, including the role of international organizations, cooperation between European countries, and the impact on foreign relations.

The strain on healthcare and welfare systems in European countries due to the influx of Arab migrants is another important consideration. The book investigates the implications for healthcare access, social services, and public expenditure. It highlights the need for adequate resources and policies to ensure the well-being of both migrants and host communities.

Education and youth integration are also key areas to explore. The section examines the challenges and opportunities related to the integration of Arab migrant youth into European education systems. It analyzes educational policies, language support, and the impact on social mobility.

Finally, media representation and public perception are addressed. The section examines how the mass migration of Arabs into Europe is portrayed in the media and analyzes the role of media in shaping public perception, stereotypes, and understanding of the issue. It emphasizes the importance of responsible and unbiased reporting to foster a more informed public discourse.

In conclusion, this section provides a comprehensive analysis of the political and social consequences of mass migration, focusing on the recent influx of Arabs into Europe. It offers insights and recommendations for policymakers to address the challenges and opportunities that arise from this migration wave.

Section 2: Economic impact: exploring the economic consequences of the mass migration of Arabs into Europe, including the effects on local job markets, wages, and economic growth.

Labor market effects: competition and displacement

The recent mass migration of Arabs into Europe has sparked concerns about the potential political and social consequences. One of the key areas of concern is the economic impact of this migration, specifically the effects on local job markets, wages, and economic growth.

As Arab migrants enter European countries, they inevitably join the labor market, competing with local workers for employment opportunities. This increased competition can have both positive and negative effects. On one hand, it can lead to a more diverse and dynamic labor force, bringing new skills and perspectives. On the other hand, it can also create challenges for local workers, especially those in low-skilled or unskilled positions, who may face displacement or downward pressure on wages.

Studies have shown that the impact of immigration on the labor market is complex and context-dependent. In some cases, immigrants can fill labor shortages and contribute to economic growth. However, in other cases, they may displace local workers, particularly those in low-skilled occupations. The extent of these effects is influenced by various factors, such as the skill levels of both immigrants and native workers, the structure of the local labor market, and the policies in place to manage immigration.

It is crucial for policymakers to carefully consider the labor market effects of Arab migration into Europe. Efforts should be made to ensure that immigrants are integrated into the labor market in a way that minimizes negative effects and maximizes the potential benefits. This can be achieved through policies that promote skills development and language acquisition among migrants, as well as measures to support the retraining and upskilling of local workers who may be at risk of displacement.

Furthermore, it is important to acknowledge that labor market effects are not solely determined by immigration. Other factors, such as technological advancements, globalization, and changes in industry structure, also play a significant role. Therefore, a comprehensive approach is needed, which takes into account not only the impact of Arab migration but also broader economic trends and challenges.

In conclusion, the mass migration of Arabs into Europe has significant implications for labor markets. Policymakers must carefully consider the potential competition and displacement effects, while also recognizing the potential benefits that a diverse labor force can bring. By implementing appropriate policies and strategies, Europe can navigate the labor market challenges posed by this migration and ensure a more inclusive and prosperous future for all.

Wage effects: impact on local workers' wages

The recent mass migration of Arabs into Europe has had significant economic consequences, particularly in relation to local job markets, wages, and economic growth. This section aims to explore the wage effects on local workers resulting from the influx of Arab migrants, providing a comprehensive understanding for policymakers.

One of the key concerns regarding the mass migration is the potential impact on wages. As Arab migrants enter the labor market, there is a possibility that they may compete with local workers for job opportunities, leading to a potential decrease in wages. However, it is essential to analyze this issue from a nuanced perspective.

Several studies have shown that the impact on local workers' wages is not uniform across all sectors and skill levels. While some sectors may experience downward pressure on wages due to increased competition, others may benefit from the new labor supply, filling gaps in the workforce and supporting economic growth. It is crucial for policymakers to recognize these variations and tailor their responses accordingly.

Furthermore, it is important to consider the long-term effects of migration on wages. Research has indicated that the overall impact on wages tends to be modest and temporary. Over time, migrants contribute to economic growth, create new jobs, and enhance productivity, leading to potential wage increases for both local workers and migrants.

To mitigate any negative wage effects, policymakers should focus on promoting skills development and education for both local workers and migrants. By investing in training programs and language support, policymakers can enhance the employability of both groups, reducing the potential for wage competition.

Additionally, it is crucial to establish effective labor market policies that ensure fair wages and protect workers' rights. This includes robust enforcement of labor laws, combating wage theft and exploitation, and promoting collective bargaining to safeguard the interests of all workers, regardless of their origin.

In conclusion, while the mass migration of Arabs into Europe may have some impact on local workers' wages, it is essential to approach this issue with nuance and evidence-based policies. By investing in skills development, promoting fair labor practices, and recognizing the positive contributions of migrants to economic growth, policymakers can mitigate any potential negative effects and foster an inclusive and prosperous society for all.

Economic growth and development: potential benefits and challenges

In the wake of the recent mass migration of Arabs into Europe, understanding the potential benefits and challenges of this phenomenon is of utmost importance for policymakers. This section aims to explore the economic consequences of this migration, including its effects on local job markets, wages, and overall economic growth.

One of the potential benefits of Arab migration is the injection of new labor into European job markets. With many Arab migrants possessing diverse skills and qualifications, they can contribute to filling labor gaps in various sectors, such as healthcare, construction, and IT. This influx of talent can lead to increased productivity and innovation, thereby boosting economic growth. Additionally, Arab migrants may also contribute to entrepreneurship and the creation of new businesses, further stimulating economic development in host countries.

However, it is essential to acknowledge the challenges that accompany this migration. The sudden increase in the labor supply can potentially impact local job markets, leading to increased competition for employment opportunities. This can result in lower wages and job insecurity for both migrants and native workers. Policymakers must address these challenges through effective labor market policies, ensuring that the benefits of migration are shared equitably among all members of society.

Integration challenges are another critical aspect to consider. Arab migrants often face social and cultural barriers, such as language differences, discrimination, and struggles with identity formation. These challenges can hinder their ability to fully integrate into European societies, impacting their economic participation and social inclusion. It is crucial for policymakers to implement inclusive integration policies that address these barriers, providing language support, anti-discrimination measures, and opportunities for cultural exchange and understanding.

Furthermore, the potential security implications of mass migration cannot be overlooked. While the majority of Arab migrants are seeking refuge from conflict and persecution, there is a risk of radicalization and terrorism. Policymakers must work closely with security agencies to ensure effective screening and monitoring processes without stigmatizing the entire migrant population. Strengthening European security systems and fostering cooperation between countries is vital for managing these security concerns.

This section will also delve into other important topics related to the migration crisis, including refugee crisis management, social cohesion and multiculturalism, political polarization and far-right movements, humanitarian response and international cooperation, healthcare and welfare systems, education and youth integration, as well as media representation and public perception. By understanding the potential benefits and challenges in each of these areas, policymakers can make informed decisions and implement effective policies to address the complex issues surrounding Arab migration into Europe.

Policy implications: addressing economic concerns and maximizing benefits

The recent mass migration of Arabs into Europe has brought with it a plethora of political and social consequences that cannot be ignored. However, one area that requires immediate attention is the economic impact of this migration. It is crucial for politicians to address economic concerns and maximize the benefits that can be derived from this influx of migrants.

One of the key concerns is the effect on local job markets. The sudden increase in the labor supply can potentially lead to a decrease in wages and job opportunities for the local population. It is essential for policymakers to devise strategies that ensure fair competition in the job market and protect the rights of both Arab migrants and local workers.

Furthermore, the economic growth of European countries may also be affected. While migrants can contribute to economic growth through their skills and entrepreneurial spirit, policymakers need to create an enabling environment that allows migrants to fully utilize their potential. This includes providing access to education and vocational training, as well as facilitating the recognition of their qualifications and skills.

Integration challenges also play a significant role in the economic impact of Arab migration. Language barriers, discrimination, and identity formation can hinder the successful integration of migrants into European societies. To address these challenges, policymakers should invest in language programs, promote cultural exchange, and enforce anti-discrimination laws.

A crucial consideration is the potential security implications of this mass migration. Policymakers must carefully assess the risk of radicalization and terrorism, while also ensuring that the strain on European security systems is managed effectively. This requires robust intelligence-sharing mechanisms, cooperation with international partners, and the development of comprehensive counter-terrorism strategies.

Additionally, the management of the refugee crisis itself has political and social consequences. It is imperative for politicians to understand the impact of their decisions on domestic politics, public opinion, and policy-making. This includes addressing concerns of the local population, engaging in transparent and inclusive decision-making processes, and implementing effective refugee integration policies.

Finally, it is essential to foster social cohesion and multiculturalism in European societies. The potential for cultural clashes and tensions necessitates the implementation of social integration policies that promote understanding, tolerance, and respect for diversity. This includes initiatives that encourage interaction between different communities, promote intercultural dialogue, and challenge stereotypes and misconceptions.

In conclusion, addressing economic concerns and maximizing the benefits of Arab migration into Europe requires a comprehensive and multi-faceted approach. Policymakers must carefully consider the impact on job markets, economic growth, integration challenges, security concerns, refugee crisis management, social cohesion, political polarization, humanitarian response, healthcare and welfare systems, education and youth integration, and media representation. By formulating effective policies in these areas, politicians can ensure a positive outcome for both Arab migrants and European societies as a whole.

Section 3: Integration challenges: examining the social and cultural integration challenges faced by Arab migrants in European societies, such as language barriers, discrimination, and identity formation.

Language barriers and access to education

Language barriers play a significant role in the access to education for Arab migrants in Europe. As politicians, it is crucial to understand the implications of these barriers and develop strategies to overcome them in order to promote integration and social mobility.

One of the main challenges faced by Arab migrant youth in European education systems is the language barrier. Many of these individuals arrive with limited proficiency in the language of the host country, making it difficult for them to fully participate in the education system. Language is not only essential for academic success but also for social integration and cultural understanding.

Without adequate language support, Arab migrant youth may struggle to communicate with their peers and teachers, leading to feelings of isolation and exclusion. Additionally, language barriers can hinder their ability to access educational resources, understand instructions, and perform well academically. This can have long-term consequences on their educational attainment and future opportunities.

To address this issue, policymakers must prioritize language support programs for Arab migrant youth. These programs should include intensive language classes, targeted support for academic vocabulary, and cultural orientation courses. It is also essential to provide resources such as bilingual teachers and interpreters to facilitate communication and understanding.

Furthermore, it is crucial to promote inclusive school environments that value and celebrate diversity. Educators should receive training on cultural sensitivity and anti-discrimination practices to ensure that Arab migrant youth feel welcomed and supported in the education system.

By addressing language barriers and promoting inclusive education, policymakers can empower Arab migrant youth to overcome social and cultural challenges. This, in turn, will contribute to their integration into European societies, enhance social cohesion, and promote multiculturalism.

It is important for politicians to recognize that investing in the education of Arab migrant youth is not only a matter of social justice but also an investment in the future. By providing them with the necessary language skills and educational opportunities, we can unlock their potential, foster their social mobility, and contribute to the economic growth and development of our societies.

In conclusion, language barriers pose significant challenges to the access to education for Arab migrants in Europe. It is the responsibility of politicians to address these barriers by implementing comprehensive language support programs, promoting inclusive school environments, and investing in the education of Arab migrant youth. By doing so, we can ensure that they have the opportunity to thrive academically, socially, and economically, ultimately contributing to the political and social stability of our societies.

Discrimination and social exclusion

The recent mass migration of Arabs into Europe has presented significant political and social challenges for policymakers. One of the key issues that must be addressed is the discrimination and social exclusion faced by Arab migrants in European societies. This section aims to shed light on the various aspects of this issue and its potential consequences.

Firstly, language barriers pose a significant challenge to the social integration of Arab migrants. Without adequate language skills, it becomes difficult for them to access education, employment, and other essential services. This further perpetuates their marginalization and hinders their ability to fully participate in European societies.

Discrimination against Arab migrants also manifests in various forms, including employment discrimination and racial profiling. This not only deprives them of equal opportunities but also fosters social exclusion and alienation. It is crucial for policymakers to implement anti-discrimination measures and promote diversity in the workforce to counter these negative effects.

Identity formation is another area of concern. Arab migrants often struggle to reconcile their cultural and religious heritage with the demands of their new environment. This internal conflict can lead to a sense of disconnection and isolation, making it imperative for societies to foster inclusive environments that allow individuals to maintain their cultural identities while also embracing their new homes.

Furthermore, the potential for radicalization and terrorism is a pressing security concern associated with the mass migration. While it is important not to conflate migration with terrorism, policymakers must be vigilant in identifying individuals who may be susceptible to extremist ideologies and provide support to prevent radicalization.

The political and social consequences of the refugee crisis management also need to be examined. The influx of Arab migrants has had a profound impact on domestic politics, public opinion, and policy-making. It is crucial for politicians to navigate these challenges in a way that upholds humanitarian principles while also addressing the concerns of their constituents.

The mass migration has also tested the social cohesion and multiculturalism of European societies. Cultural clashes and tensions may arise, necessitating the implementation of social integration policies that promote understanding, tolerance, and respect among different communities.

The rise of far-right political movements and parties in response to the mass migration is a concerning development. These movements often exploit anti-immigrant sentiments, further exacerbating divisions within societies. Understanding their platforms, rhetoric, and impact on European politics is essential for effective policymaking.

International cooperation and humanitarian response are crucial in managing the migration crisis. The political and social consequences of the international community's response to the crisis, including the role of international organizations and cooperation between European countries, must be analyzed to identify areas for improvement and collaboration.

The strain on healthcare and welfare systems due to the influx of Arab migrants is another important consideration. Policymakers must evaluate the implications for healthcare access, social services, and public expenditure to ensure the sustainability and fairness of these systems.

Lastly, the media plays a significant role in shaping public perception, stereotypes, and understanding of the mass migration issue. It is essential to critically examine how the media portrays Arab migrants and their experiences to counter misinformation and promote a more informed and empathetic public discourse.

In conclusion, discrimination and social exclusion are important aspects to consider regarding the mass migration of Arabs into Europe. Policymakers must address the challenges faced by Arab migrants in terms of language, discrimination, identity formation, and security concerns. Furthermore, the impact on social cohesion, politics, healthcare, education, and media representation all require careful analysis and consideration to ensure the effective management of the migration crisis and the promotion of inclusive and cohesive societies.

Identity formation and cultural clashes

The recent mass migration of Arabs into Europe has brought to light the complex issue of identity formation and cultural clashes. As these individuals seek to integrate into European societies, they face numerous challenges that impact their sense of self and their ability to adapt to their new surroundings. This section aims to explore these challenges and their potential political and social consequences.

One of the key issues faced by Arab migrants in Europe is the formation of their identity. The clash between their cultural heritage and the dominant European culture poses a significant challenge. Language barriers, discrimination, and a sense of alienation can hinder the process of identity formation and contribute to feelings of marginalization. It is crucial for policymakers to understand these challenges and develop strategies to promote social and cultural integration.

Cultural clashes are another significant concern. The collision of different values, norms, and traditions can lead to tensions and conflicts within European societies. This has the potential to strain social cohesion and multiculturalism. It is imperative for policymakers to address these cultural clashes through dialogue, education, and the promotion of intercultural understanding.

Furthermore, the potential for radicalization and security implications cannot be overlooked. While the majority of Arab migrants are seeking safety and a better life, a small fraction may be vulnerable to radical ideologies. This poses a significant security risk, as it can lead to instances of terrorism and strain European security systems. Policymakers must prioritize security measures while also addressing the root causes of radicalization.

The management of the refugee crisis also has political and social consequences. The influx of Arab migrants has had a profound impact on domestic politics, public opinion, and policy-making. The rise of far-right movements and political polarization in response to the mass migration is a testament to the challenges faced by policymakers. It is vital to find a balance between humanitarian response and national interests, while also considering the long-term implications of the chosen policies.

The strain on healthcare and welfare systems is another concern. The influx of Arab migrants has increased the demand for healthcare services and social welfare. Policymakers must address the strain on these systems and allocate resources effectively to ensure that both the migrants and the local population have access to essential services.

Education and youth integration also present challenges and opportunities. Arab migrant youth face barriers to education, such as language support and cultural differences. Policymakers should focus on providing inclusive educational policies that promote social mobility and empower these young individuals to contribute positively to European societies.

Lastly, media representation and public perception play a significant role in shaping attitudes towards Arab migrants. The portrayal of the mass migration in the media can perpetuate stereotypes and misunderstandings. Policymakers should work towards promoting accurate and balanced media coverage to foster understanding and empathy among the public.

In conclusion, the issues of identity formation and cultural clashes are critical considerations for policymakers in addressing the mass migration of Arabs into Europe. By understanding and addressing these challenges, policymakers can work towards creating inclusive societies that embrace diversity and promote social integration.

Integration policies and best practices

Integration policies and best practices play a crucial role in addressing the complex challenges that arise from the recent mass migration of Arabs into Europe. As politicians, it is imperative to understand and implement effective strategies to ensure the successful integration of Arab migrants into European societies. This section will explore various integration policies and best practices that can help navigate the potential political and social consequences of this migration wave.

One crucial aspect to consider is the economic impact of this mass migration. It is essential to analyze the effects on local job markets, wages, and economic growth. By providing opportunities for skill development and employment, integration policies can help mitigate any negative economic consequences and promote the economic contribution of Arab migrants.

Another area of concern is the social and cultural integration challenges faced by Arab migrants in European societies. Language barriers, discrimination, and identity formation are key obstacles that need to be addressed. Integration policies should focus on providing language support, promoting cultural exchange programs, and combating discrimination to foster social cohesion.

Security concerns are also paramount, requiring a comprehensive analysis of the potential risk of radicalization and terrorism. Integration policies should include measures for effective integration and counter-terrorism strategies, such as promoting community engagement, education, and social inclusion.

The management of the refugee crisis is another critical aspect to consider. European countries' handling of the crisis can have profound political and social consequences. Policies should focus on ensuring a fair and efficient asylum process, balancing domestic politics, public opinion, and policy-making to ensure the well-being of both migrants and host communities.

The influx of Arab migrants also has implications for social cohesion and multiculturalism. Policies should aim to address cultural clashes and tensions by promoting intercultural dialogue, understanding, and respect. Social integration policies, such as access to education and housing, can also contribute to fostering multicultural societies.

The rise of far-right movements in response to the mass migration poses a challenge to European politics. Understanding their platforms, rhetoric, and impact is crucial for developing inclusive policies that address the concerns of all citizens and promote social harmony.

International cooperation and humanitarian response are essential in managing the migration crisis. Collaboration between European countries and international organizations can help ensure a coordinated and effective response, while also considering the impact on foreign relations.

The strain on healthcare and welfare systems due to the influx of Arab migrants necessitates an examination of the implications for healthcare access, social services, and public expenditure. Adequate funding and resource allocation are vital to ensure the provision of quality healthcare and welfare support.

Education plays a significant role in the integration of Arab migrant youth. Policies should focus on providing language support, culturally sensitive education, and opportunities for social mobility. By investing in education, we can empower the next generation and foster their integration into European societies.

Lastly, media representation and public perception play a crucial role in shaping attitudes towards the mass migration of Arabs into Europe. Analyzing the role of media in portraying this issue, challenging stereotypes, and promoting a more nuanced understanding is essential for fostering empathy, understanding, and social cohesion.

In conclusion, integration policies and best practices are vital in addressing the political and social consequences of the mass migration of Arabs into Europe. By implementing effective strategies in areas such as economics, education, security, and social cohesion, politicians can navigate the challenges and promote the successful integration of Arab migrants into European societies.

Section 4: Security concerns: analyzing the potential security implications of the mass migration, including the risk of radicalization, terrorism, and the strain on European security systems.

Radicalization and extremism: addressing the root causes

In recent years, Europe has witnessed a significant influx of Arab migrants, leading to a multitude of political and social consequences. One of the most pressing issues that policymakers must grapple with is the potential for radicalization and extremism among these newcomers. Understanding and addressing the root causes of this phenomenon is crucial in order to prevent the spread of violence and ensure the safety and security of European societies.

Radicalization and extremism are complex issues that require a multifaceted approach. While it is important to tackle the immediate threats posed by extremist groups, it is equally important to address the underlying factors that contribute to radicalization. Poverty, marginalization, social exclusion, and a lack of opportunities are often cited as key drivers of extremism. As such, policymakers should focus on creating inclusive societies that provide equal opportunities for all, regardless of their background.

Education plays a crucial role in countering radicalization. By promoting critical thinking, tolerance, and respect for diversity, educational institutions can help prevent the spread of extremist ideologies. Additionally, investing in language support programs and integrating Arab migrant youth into European education systems can foster social integration and empower these individuals to become active members of their communities.

Another important aspect to consider is the role of media in shaping public perception and understanding of the Arab migration issue. Negative stereotypes and sensationalized reporting can contribute to a climate of fear and hostility. It is imperative for policymakers to work with media outlets to ensure accurate and balanced coverage, promoting a more nuanced understanding of the challenges and opportunities presented by the migration crisis.

Furthermore, addressing the root causes of radicalization requires international cooperation. European countries must work together, along with international organizations, to share best practices and develop comprehensive strategies that tackle the issue from its core. This includes cooperation in intelligence sharing, border control, and the exchange of information on extremist networks.

Ultimately, addressing the root causes of radicalization and extremism among Arab migrants is not only a matter of security, but also a social and humanitarian imperative. By creating inclusive societies, investing in education, promoting accurate media representation, and fostering international cooperation, policymakers can mitigate the risks associated with radicalization and ensure the successful integration of Arab migrants into European societies.

Terrorism and security threats: assessing the risks

As Europe faces an unprecedented mass migration of Arabs, it is crucial for policymakers to assess the potential security threats that may arise from this situation. This section delves into the various risks associated with terrorism and security concerns, providing an in-depth analysis for politicians to understand the complexities at hand.

The mass migration of Arabs into Europe has raised legitimate concerns about the potential for radicalization and terrorism. While it is essential not to stigmatize an entire community, policymakers must acknowledge the risk and develop effective strategies to mitigate it. This section examines the factors that contribute to radicalization, such as social exclusion, economic marginalization, and the influence of extremist ideologies.

Furthermore, it explores the strain on European security systems caused by the influx of migrants. Policymakers need to assess the adequacy of existing security measures and consider the need for additional resources and cooperation between nations to ensure the safety of their citizens.

The section also delves into the challenges faced by intelligence agencies in identifying and preventing potential terrorist threats within migrant communities. It highlights the importance of cultural understanding, community engagement, and intelligence sharing in effectively combating terrorism.

Additionally, it addresses the need for comprehensive screening processes and effective border control measures to prevent the entry of individuals with malicious intent. Policymakers must strike a balance between humanitarian concerns and security imperatives, ensuring that the screening process is thorough but not discriminatory.

To effectively address these security concerns, this section provides recommendations for policymakers. It emphasizes the importance of investing in integration programs that promote social cohesion, cultural understanding, and economic opportunities for Arab migrants. Furthermore, it stresses the need for improved cooperation between European countries, intelligence agencies, and international organizations to share information and coordinate efforts in countering terrorism.

By understanding and assessing the risks associated with the mass migration of Arabs into Europe, policymakers can make informed decisions to ensure the safety and security of their nations. It is crucial that politicians approach this issue with a balanced perspective, recognizing the potential security threats without succumbing to fear or discrimination. With effective policies and proactive measures, Europe can navigate this challenging period and foster a harmonious coexistence between its citizens and the new arrivals.

Strain on European security systems: capacity and resources

The recent mass migration of Arabs into Europe has brought about significant political and social consequences, one of which is the strain on European security systems. As politicians, it is crucial to understand the capacity and resources needed to address the potential security implications of this mass migration.

The influx of Arab migrants poses various security concerns that must be carefully analyzed. One of the key risks is the potential for radicalization and terrorism. While it is important to recognize that the vast majority of Arab migrants are seeking refuge and a better life, there is a small minority that may be susceptible to extremist ideologies. This minority must be identified and appropriately dealt with to prevent any security threats.

Another aspect of the strain on European security systems is the sheer scale of the migration. The influx of such a large number of people puts pressure on existing resources, such as law enforcement agencies, border control, and intelligence services. Policymakers must ensure that these security systems are adequately equipped and staffed to handle the increased workload effectively.

Moreover, the strain on European security systems also extends to the coordination and cooperation between countries. The mass migration has highlighted the need for enhanced international collaboration to share intelligence, exchange information, and track potential threats across borders. It is imperative for politicians to foster strong relationships and cooperation mechanisms to effectively manage security challenges arising from the migration crisis.

Furthermore, the strain on European security systems also has financial implications. Allocating resources to address security concerns, including counter-terrorism efforts and intelligence gathering, requires significant investment. Policymakers must consider the financial burden of these additional security measures and ensure that adequate funding is allocated to support the capacity-building and resource needs of security agencies.

In conclusion, the mass migration of Arabs into Europe has placed a strain on European security systems. Policymakers must recognize the potential security implications, including the risks of radicalization and terrorism, and take appropriate measures to address these concerns. This requires sufficient capacity and resources in terms of law enforcement, border control, intelligence services, and international cooperation. By understanding and effectively managing these challenges, politicians can ensure the safety and security of European societies while also addressing the political and social consequences of the migration crisis.

Cooperation and intelligence sharing: mitigating security challenges

In the face of the recent mass migration of Arabs into Europe, it is crucial for politicians to address the potential security challenges that may arise. Cooperation and intelligence sharing between European countries is essential in mitigating these challenges and ensuring the safety and well-being of both the migrants and the host societies.

The influx of Arab migrants brings with it concerns about potential radicalization and terrorism. As such, it is imperative for European countries to work together in sharing intelligence on individuals who may pose a security risk. By pooling their resources and expertise, countries can effectively identify and monitor potential threats, preventing any potential acts of violence or radicalization.

Additionally, the strain on European security systems cannot be ignored. The large number of migrants entering the continent places a burden on law enforcement agencies, border control, and intelligence services. By fostering cooperation and sharing best practices, European countries can better manage their resources and ensure the efficient functioning of their security systems.

Cooperation should extend beyond European borders as well. The international community must play a role in addressing the security implications of the mass migration. International organizations can offer support and guidance to European countries, facilitating cooperation and intelligence sharing on a global scale. Furthermore, cooperation with the countries of origin can prove vital in preventing further security challenges. By working closely with Arab nations, European countries can better understand the motivations behind migration and address any potential issues at their source.

However, cooperation and intelligence sharing alone are not enough. It is equally important for politicians to invest in the social integration of Arab migrants. By addressing the root causes of radicalization and offering opportunities for education, employment, and community engagement, European societies can foster a sense of belonging and reduce the risk of social unrest.

In conclusion, the mass migration of Arabs into Europe presents significant security challenges that must be addressed by politicians. By prioritizing cooperation and intelligence sharing, both within Europe and internationally, politicians can work towards mitigating risks and ensuring the safety of all individuals. Simultaneously, efforts must be made to promote social integration, providing opportunities for the migrants to thrive within European societies. Only through a comprehensive approach can the potential security challenges be effectively managed.

Section 5: Refugee crisis management: exploring the political and social consequences of how European countries are managing the refugee crisis, including the impact on domestic politics, public opinion, and policy-making.

Domestic politics and party dynamics

Domestic politics and party dynamics play a crucial role in shaping the response to the recent mass migration of Arabs into Europe. As politicians, it is essential to understand the potential political and social consequences of this migration and how it affects various aspects of European society.

One key area to consider is the economic impact of Arab migration. It is important to explore the effects on local job markets, wages, and economic growth. While some argue that migrants contribute to economic growth through their labor, others express concerns about job displacement and wage depression. Understanding these dynamics is crucial for effective policymaking.

Integration challenges faced by Arab migrants in European societies also demand attention. Language barriers, discrimination, and identity formation are key hurdles that need to be addressed for successful integration. Policymakers must consider the importance of social and cultural integration policies to ensure the inclusion of migrants and prevent the formation of isolated communities.

The potential security implications of the mass migration cannot be ignored. The risk of radicalization, terrorism, and strain on European security systems must be carefully evaluated. Policymakers should work towards effective screening and integration processes to mitigate these risks while ensuring the safety and security of all citizens.

Refugee crisis management is another critical aspect to explore. The political and social consequences of how European countries are managing the crisis are far-reaching. The impact on domestic politics, public opinion, and policy-making cannot be underestimated. Understanding these consequences will aid in developing more effective and informed responses to the crisis.

The mass migration of Arabs into Europe also has implications for social cohesion and multiculturalism. Cultural clashes and tensions may arise, highlighting the need for social integration policies. Policymakers should strive towards fostering social cohesion and promoting multiculturalism while addressing potential conflicts.

Furthermore, the rise of far-right political movements and parties in response to the mass migration needs comprehensive study. Analyzing their platforms, rhetoric, and impact on European politics is crucial for addressing political polarization and maintaining social stability.

International cooperation and humanitarian response also play a significant role. Understanding the consequences of the international community's response to the migration crisis, including the role of international organizations and cooperation between European countries, is vital for effective policymaking and foreign relations.

The strain on healthcare and welfare systems in European countries due to the influx of Arab migrants must be investigated. Policymakers need to analyze the implications for healthcare access, social services, and public expenditure to ensure the well-being of both migrants and European citizens.

Lastly, the challenges and opportunities related to the integration of Arab migrant youth into European education systems deserve attention. Examining educational policies, language support, and the impact on social mobility will aid in the successful integration and empowerment of the younger generation.

Media representation and public perception also play a crucial role in shaping attitudes towards the mass migration. Analyzing the role of media in shaping public perception, stereotypes, and understanding of the issue is essential for countering misinformation and promoting informed discussions.

In conclusion, understanding domestic politics and party dynamics is vital for addressing the political and social consequences of the mass migration of Arabs into Europe. By exploring these various aspects, policymakers can develop effective strategies to manage the crisis, promote integration, and ensure the well-being of both migrants and European citizens.

Public opinion and backlash

The recent mass migration of Arabs into Europe has sparked significant public opinion and backlash, which has had profound political and social consequences. As politicians, it is crucial to understand and address these concerns in order to effectively manage the situation and mitigate any negative impacts.

One of the key areas of concern is the economic impact of the mass migration. Many European citizens worry about the effects on local job markets, wages, and economic growth. It is essential to examine these concerns and develop policies that ensure the fair distribution of resources and opportunities for both the native population and the Arab migrants. This will help alleviate public anxiety and promote social cohesion.

Integration challenges are another important aspect to consider. Arab migrants often face social and cultural integration challenges, such as language barriers, discrimination, and identity formation. Policymakers must develop comprehensive integration programs that address these challenges and promote inclusivity. By fostering a sense of belonging and offering support, European societies can create an environment where Arab migrants can thrive and contribute to the host countries.

Security concerns also arise from the mass migration, with potential risks of radicalization, terrorism, and strain on European security systems. It is vital to analyze these security implications and develop effective strategies to prevent and counter any threats. Cooperation between European countries and international organizations is crucial to address these concerns and ensure the safety of both migrants and host communities.

The political and social consequences of how European countries manage the refugee crisis are also significant. This includes the impact on domestic politics, public opinion, and policy-making. It is imperative to handle the crisis in a way that is transparent, fair, and aligns with the values of the European Union. This will help maintain public trust and ensure the continuation of effective policies.

The mass migration of Arabs into Europe has also had an impact on social cohesion and multiculturalism. Cultural clashes and tensions can arise, highlighting the need for social integration policies. By promoting mutual understanding and respect, European societies can embrace diversity and foster social cohesion.

Furthermore, the rise of far-right political movements and parties in response to the mass migration must be studied. It is important to understand their platforms, rhetoric, and impact on European politics. By addressing the concerns that fuel their rise, politicians can work towards a more inclusive and tolerant society.

International cooperation and the humanitarian response to the migration crisis are also crucial factors to consider. Policymakers must analyze the political and social consequences of the international community's response, including the role of international organizations and the impact on foreign relations.

The strain on healthcare and welfare systems in European countries is another concern. The influx of Arab migrants may impact healthcare access, social services, and public expenditure. It is essential to develop strategies that ensure the sustainability and equitable distribution of resources.

Finally, media representation and public perception play a significant role in shaping attitudes towards the mass migration of Arabs into Europe. Policymakers must critically analyze media portrayals and work towards countering stereotypes and promoting a more nuanced understanding of the issue.

In conclusion, public opinion and backlash surrounding the mass migration of Arabs into Europe have wide-ranging political and social consequences. As politicians, it is our responsibility to address these concerns and develop effective policies that foster integration, ensure security, and promote social cohesion. By doing so, we can embrace the potential of Arab migrants and create a more inclusive and prosperous Europe.

Policy-making and decision-making processes

Policy-making and decision-making processes play a crucial role in addressing the political and social consequences of the recent mass migration of Arabs into Europe. This section explores the various dimensions of this complex issue, providing valuable insights and recommendations for policymakers.

One of the key areas of concern is the economic impact of this migration. Policymakers need to carefully examine the effects on local job markets, wages, and economic growth. By understanding these consequences, they can develop effective policies to mitigate any negative effects and harness the potential benefits that migration can bring to the economy.

Integration challenges faced by Arab migrants in European societies are another pressing issue. Policymakers must address language barriers, discrimination, and identity formation, to ensure the successful integration of these migrants. By implementing comprehensive integration policies, they can create inclusive societies and promote social and cultural cohesion.

Security concerns also demand policymakers' attention. They must analyze the potential risks of radicalization, terrorism, and the strain on European security systems. By developing robust security measures and fostering cooperation between countries, policymakers can ensure the safety and well-being of both migrants and host communities.

The management of the refugee crisis is another critical aspect. Policymakers must carefully consider the political and social consequences of their decisions. They should take into account the impact on domestic politics, public opinion, and policy-making, while ensuring that humanitarian principles guide their actions.

The Arab migration also poses challenges to social cohesion and multiculturalism in European societies. Policymakers must address potential cultural clashes and tensions through the implementation of effective social integration policies. This will help foster a harmonious coexistence and promote multiculturalism as a strength rather than a source of conflict.

The rise of far-right political movements and parties in response to the mass migration is a concerning trend. Policymakers must study their platforms, rhetoric, and impact on European politics. By understanding the root causes of this polarization, they can develop strategies to counteract it and promote inclusive and tolerant societies.

Furthermore, the international community's response to the migration crisis has significant political and social consequences. Policymakers need to analyze the role of international organizations, cooperation between European countries, and the impact on foreign relations. By fostering humanitarian response and international cooperation, they can effectively address the challenges posed by this migration.

The strain on healthcare and welfare systems in European countries due to the influx of Arab migrants is another important consideration. Policymakers must investigate the implications for healthcare access, social services, and public expenditure. By developing sustainable and equitable healthcare and welfare policies, they can ensure that both migrants and host communities receive the support they need.

Education and youth integration are also crucial aspects. Policymakers must understand the challenges and opportunities related to the integration of Arab migrant youth into European education systems. They should develop educational policies that provide language support and promote social mobility, ensuring that these young individuals have equal opportunities for success.

Lastly, media representation and public perception play a significant role in shaping the discourse around this migration. Policymakers must critically examine how the mass migration of Arabs into Europe is portrayed in the media. By promoting accurate and balanced reporting, they can challenge stereotypes, foster understanding, and promote empathy towards migrants.

In conclusion, policymakers must navigate a complex landscape of political and social consequences when addressing the mass migration of Arabs into Europe. By understanding and addressing these key issues, they can develop effective policies that promote integration, social cohesion, and economic prosperity, while ensuring the safety and well-being of both migrants and host communities.

Lessons learned and future directions

The recent mass migration of Arabs into Europe has undoubtedly been a political and social wake-up call for politicians across the continent. As policymakers grapple with the multifaceted consequences of this migration wave, it is imperative to reflect on the lessons learned and chart a course for future directions. This section explores the key areas that demand attention from political leaders in order to effectively address the challenges posed by the Arab migration into Europe.

One of the most pressing concerns is the economic impact of this influx. Policymakers must carefully examine the effects on local job markets, wages, and overall economic growth. It is crucial to strike a balance between addressing the needs of Arab migrants and safeguarding the interests of local communities. This may require implementing policies that promote job creation, vocational training, and entrepreneurship among both migrant and local populations.

Integration challenges also loom large. Language barriers, discrimination, and identity formation are formidable obstacles faced by Arab migrants in European societies. Politicians must prioritize social and cultural integration by investing in language support programs, promoting diversity and tolerance, and combating discrimination.

Moreover, fostering a sense of belonging and shared values is essential to ensure social cohesion and prevent cultural clashes.

Security concerns cannot be overlooked. The potential risk of radicalization and terrorism must be addressed through comprehensive approaches that encompass intelligence sharing, cooperation among security agencies, and targeted counter-radicalization programs. Strengthening European security systems and enhancing border control measures are equally vital to maintain public safety.

Refugee crisis management is another critical area demanding attention. Politicians must carefully navigate the political and social consequences of managing the refugee crisis. This includes considering the impact on domestic politics, public opinion, and policy-making. Striking a balance between humanitarian obligations and national interests is paramount.

The impact on social cohesion and multiculturalism cannot be underestimated. Politicians should promote dialogue, understanding, and acceptance among diverse communities. Developing effective social integration policies and fostering intercultural exchange programs can foster mutual respect and appreciation.

The rise of far-right movements in response to the mass migration necessitates careful analysis. Understanding their platforms, rhetoric, and impact on European politics is crucial to effectively counter their divisive narratives and protect democratic values.

Humanitarian response and international cooperation are vital. Policymakers must assess the consequences of the international community's response to the migration crisis, including the role of international organizations, cooperation between European countries, and the impact on foreign relations.

The strain on healthcare and welfare systems must not be overlooked. Policymakers must ensure access to healthcare and social services for both migrants and local populations, while also managing public expenditure effectively.

Lastly, education and youth integration must be prioritized. Policies should focus on addressing the challenges faced by Arab migrant youth in European education systems, including language support and social mobility opportunities.

The media's role in shaping public perception, stereotypes, and understanding of the Arab migration issue cannot be understated. Policymakers should encourage balanced reporting, counter misinformation, and promote a nuanced understanding of the complexities involved.

In conclusion, the lessons learned from the Arab migration into Europe provide valuable insights for policymakers. By addressing the economic, social, security, and humanitarian dimensions, politicians can navigate the challenges effectively and shape a future that fosters integration, upholds democratic values, and ensures the well-being of both migrants and host communities.

Section 6: Social cohesion and multiculturalism: examining the effects of the Arab migration on social cohesion and multiculturalism in European societies, including the potential for cultural clashes, tensions, and the need for social integration policies.

Cultural clashes and tensions: navigating diversity

In the wake of the recent mass migration of Arabs into Europe, navigating diversity has become a pressing concern for politicians. The influx of Arab migrants has brought about various political and social consequences that need to be addressed. This section will delve into the challenges and potential solutions for managing cultural clashes and tensions in European societies.

One of the primary integration challenges faced by Arab migrants is the cultural and social divide. Language barriers, discrimination, and identity formation pose significant obstacles to their successful integration. Language proficiency programs and cultural sensitivity training can help bridge this gap and foster a sense of belonging for migrants in their host countries.

However, the mass migration also raises security concerns. The risk of radicalization and terrorism looms large, necessitating a comprehensive analysis of potential security implications. European security systems need to be strengthened to effectively address these challenges, while also ensuring the protection of individual rights and freedoms.

Refugee crisis management is another vital aspect that requires attention. The political and social consequences of how European countries handle the refugee crisis have a significant impact on domestic politics, public opinion, and policy-making. Effective management strategies must strike a balance between humanitarian concerns and national interests to maintain stability and harmony.

Social cohesion and multiculturalism are crucial for a harmonious society. The influx of Arab migrants has the potential to create cultural clashes and tensions. It is essential to develop robust social integration policies that promote understanding, respect, and acceptance among diverse communities. These policies should emphasize mutual cultural exchange and celebration of diversity.

The rise of far-right movements and political polarization is a concerning trend in response to the mass migration. Understanding their platforms, rhetoric, and impact on European politics is crucial for effectively addressing their concerns through inclusive policies and platforms that promote dialogue and cooperation.

International cooperation and humanitarian response play a significant role in managing the migration crisis. Collaboration between European countries and international organizations is essential for developing comprehensive strategies, sharing resources, and ensuring a coordinated response. The impact of these efforts on foreign relations should also be analyzed.

The strain on healthcare and welfare systems due to the influx of Arab migrants is a practical concern. Analyzing the implications for healthcare access, social services, and public expenditure is necessary to ensure the sustainability of these systems and equitable distribution of resources.

Education and youth integration are vital for the long-term success of Arab migrant youth in European societies. Examining educational policies, providing language support, and promoting social mobility can empower these individuals and contribute to their successful integration.

Lastly, media representation and public perception play a significant role in shaping attitudes toward the mass migration. Analyzing the portrayal of Arabs in the media, and the role of media in shaping public perception, stereotypes, and understanding of the issue is crucial for promoting empathy, dispelling misconceptions, and fostering dialogue.

In conclusion, navigating diversity in the context of the mass migration of Arabs into Europe requires a comprehensive understanding of the challenges and potential solutions. This section addresses the cultural clashes and tensions that arise from the migration crisis, emphasizing the need for social integration policies, security measures, and inclusive political strategies to ensure a harmonious and inclusive society.

Social integration policies: promoting cohesion

As the recent mass migration of Arabs into Europe continues to shape the political and social landscape, it is crucial for politicians to address the challenges and consequences that arise from this phenomenon. One key aspect that demands attention is the promotion of social integration policies to foster cohesion within European societies.

The influx of Arab migrants brings with it a range of social and cultural integration challenges. Language barriers, discrimination, and identity formation are issues that must be effectively addressed to ensure the successful integration of these individuals into their new communities. Language support programs, cultural awareness training, and anti-discrimination policies can play a vital role in bridging the gap and promoting a sense of belonging for Arab migrants.

Furthermore, the potential security implications of the mass migration cannot be overlooked. The risk of radicalization and terrorism poses a significant challenge to European security systems. It is essential for politicians to formulate comprehensive strategies that address these concerns while avoiding stigmatization or further marginalization of Arab migrants.

The management of the refugee crisis also has profound political and social consequences. European countries must carefully navigate the impact on domestic politics, public opinion, and policy-making. Effective refugee crisis management requires a delicate balance between humanitarian concerns and national interests.

The Arab migration also has implications for social cohesion and multiculturalism within European societies. The potential for cultural clashes and tensions necessitates the implementation of social integration policies that foster mutual understanding and respect. By promoting intercultural dialogue, community engagement, and inclusive policies, politicians can facilitate the creation of harmonious and cohesive societies.

However, it is important to consider the rise of far-right political movements and parties in response to the mass migration. The platforms and rhetoric of these movements have the potential to polarize European politics and undermine social cohesion. Politicians must address the concerns of these movements while upholding democratic values and promoting inclusive policies.

The international community's response to the migration crisis also carries political and social consequences. The role of international organizations, cooperation between European countries, and the impact on foreign relations must be carefully examined. Effective humanitarian response and international cooperation are vital in addressing the root causes of migration and finding sustainable solutions.

Additionally, the strain on healthcare and welfare systems in European countries due to the influx of Arab migrants cannot be ignored. Politicians must allocate resources and develop policies that ensure healthcare access, social services, and public expenditure are managed effectively to mitigate any negative impact on these systems.

Lastly, the integration of Arab migrant youth into European education systems presents both challenges and opportunities. Educational policies that provide language support, cultural sensitivity training, and opportunities for social mobility are essential in fostering their successful integration.

The media also plays a crucial role in shaping public perception, stereotypes, and understanding of the mass migration. Politicians must engage with media representatives to ensure accurate and balanced representation, fostering a more informed and empathetic public discourse.

In conclusion, the mass migration of Arabs into Europe poses significant political and social challenges. By promoting social integration policies that address language barriers, discrimination, and identity formation, politicians can foster cohesion within European societies. It is crucial to effectively manage the security concerns, navigate the refugee crisis, uphold multiculturalism, address far-right movements, promote international cooperation, manage healthcare and welfare systems, and facilitate the integration of Arab migrant youth. By doing so, politicians can mitigate potential conflicts and build inclusive and harmonious societies.

Strengthening multiculturalism: embracing diversity

In today's globalized world, the recent mass migration of Arabs into Europe has posed significant political and social challenges for politicians. As policymakers, it is essential to address these challenges head-on and develop strategies to strengthen multiculturalism and embrace diversity in European societies.

One of the key concerns regarding the mass migration of Arabs into Europe is the potential political and social consequences. It is crucial for politicians to understand and analyze the long-term impact of this migration on their respective countries. By studying the economic consequences, such as the effects on local job markets, wages, and economic growth, politicians can make informed decisions to mitigate any negative effects and harness the positive aspects of this migration.

Integration challenges faced by Arab migrants in European societies cannot be overlooked. Language barriers, discrimination, and identity formation are significant obstacles that need to be addressed through targeted policies and support systems. By investing in language support programs, promoting cultural awareness, and fostering social integration, politicians can ensure a smoother transition for Arab migrants into European societies.

Security concerns are another crucial aspect that politicians must consider. Analyzing the potential security implications, including the risk of radicalization, terrorism, and strain on European security systems, is imperative. By implementing comprehensive security measures, enhancing intelligence sharing between countries, and tackling the root causes of radicalization, politicians can safeguard both the migrant population and their own citizens.

The management of the refugee crisis is a pressing issue that demands attention. Politicians must carefully consider the political and social consequences of their response to this crisis, including its impact on domestic politics, public opinion, and policy-making. By adopting a humanitarian approach, promoting empathy, and collaborating with international organizations, politicians can address the crisis effectively while upholding their values and principles.

The influx of Arab migrants has significantly affected social cohesion and multiculturalism in European societies. Cultural clashes and tensions are inevitable, but politicians can mitigate these issues by implementing social integration policies, fostering intercultural dialogue, and promoting diversity. By emphasizing the benefits of multiculturalism and countering divisive narratives, politicians can foster a more inclusive and harmonious society.

The rise of far-right political movements and parties in response to the mass migration is a concerning trend. Understanding their platforms, rhetoric, and impact on European politics is crucial for politicians. By addressing the underlying concerns of the population, promoting dialogue, and offering alternative solutions, politicians can counter the polarization and extremism that arise from this migration.

Finally, the international community's response to the migration crisis must be analyzed. The role of international organizations, cooperation between European countries, and the impact on foreign relations are all significant factors. By promoting humanitarianism, strengthening international cooperation, and engaging in constructive dialogue, politicians can shape a more comprehensive and effective response to the crisis.

The mass migration of Arabs into Europe has also placed strain on healthcare and welfare systems. By carefully assessing the implications for healthcare access, social services, and public expenditure, politicians can allocate resources effectively and ensure that the needs of both the migrants and the host population are met.

Education and youth integration are vital for the successful integration of Arab migrant youth into European societies. By implementing inclusive educational policies, providing language support, and promoting social mobility, politicians can empower the younger generation and foster a sense of belonging.

Lastly, the role of media in shaping public perception of the mass migration cannot be ignored. Politicians must critically examine the portrayal of Arabs in the media, challenge stereotypes, and promote a more nuanced understanding of the issue. By engaging with the media, promoting responsible journalism, and countering misinformation, politicians can shape public opinion and create a more inclusive narrative.

In conclusion, the mass migration of Arabs into Europe presents both challenges and opportunities for politicians. By addressing the various aspects discussed in this section, politicians can strengthen multiculturalism, embrace diversity, and ensure a more inclusive and harmonious future for European societies.

Section 7: Political polarization and far-right movements: studying the rise of far-right political movements and parties in response to the mass migration, examining their platforms, rhetoric, and impact on European politics.

Rise of far-right movements: origins and ideologies

In recent years, the mass migration of Arabs into Europe has sparked the rise of far-right movements across the continent. These movements, characterized by their nationalist and anti-immigrant ideologies, have gained traction by exploiting fears and concerns surrounding the influx of Arab migrants. Understanding the origins and ideologies of these far-right movements is crucial for politicians and policymakers in order to effectively address the political and social consequences they present.

The rise of far-right movements can be traced back to a variety of factors. Economic uncertainty, job insecurity, and stagnant wages have contributed to a sense of frustration and resentment among certain segments of the European population. Far-right movements have capitalized on these grievances by presenting Arab migrants as a threat to local job markets and economic growth. By scapegoating migrants, these movements offer a simple solution to complex economic problems, thereby gaining support from those who feel left behind by globalization.

Ideologically, far-right movements espouse a nationalist agenda that seeks to preserve the cultural and ethnic identity of European nations. They argue that the mass migration of Arabs poses a threat to national cohesion and social harmony. These movements often employ xenophobic rhetoric, emphasizing the differences between Arab migrants and the native population. By stoking fears of cultural clashes and the erosion of national values, far-right movements appeal to those who feel their identity is under threat.

The impact of far-right movements on European politics cannot be underestimated. Their rise has led to a polarization of political discourse, with mainstream parties being forced to adopt more hardline stances on immigration in order to compete for voters. This shift has had significant consequences for policy-making, as politicians are pressured to enact stricter immigration laws and border controls. Moreover, the rhetoric of far-right movements has contributed to a toxic atmosphere of intolerance and discrimination, exacerbating social tensions and undermining social cohesion.

To address the rise of far-right movements, politicians must adopt a multi-faceted approach. This includes implementing policies that address the economic concerns of the population, such as promoting job creation and ensuring fair wages. Additionally, efforts must be made to foster social integration and combat discrimination faced by Arab migrants. Education plays a vital role in promoting understanding and tolerance, and policies should be implemented to support the integration of Arab migrant youth into European education systems.

Furthermore, politicians must challenge the narratives propagated by far-right movements through media representation and public perception. By promoting accurate and balanced portrayals of the Arab migration, the media can help dispel stereotypes and counteract the fear-mongering tactics employed by far-right groups.

In conclusion, the rise of far-right movements in response to the mass migration of Arabs into Europe is a pressing issue that demands the attention of politicians and policymakers. By understanding the origins and ideologies of these movements, politicians can develop effective strategies to address the political and social consequences they present. Collaboration between European nations, international organizations, and the media is essential in order to mitigate the impact of far-right movements and promote a cohesive and inclusive society.

Political rhetoric and public discourse

Political rhetoric and public discourse play a crucial role in shaping the response to the recent mass migration of Arabs into Europe. As politicians, it is essential to understand the potential political and social consequences of this migration in order to develop effective policies and strategies.

One significant aspect to consider is the economic impact of this mass migration. It is important to explore how the influx of Arab migrants affects local job markets, wages, and overall economic growth. Understanding these consequences will allow policymakers to implement measures that maximize the benefits and minimize the potential negative impacts on the economy.

Integration challenges are another critical aspect to address. Arab migrants face social and cultural integration challenges in European societies, such as language barriers, discrimination, and identity formation. Policymakers must recognize these obstacles and develop inclusive policies that promote social cohesion and cultural understanding.

Furthermore, security concerns must be carefully analyzed. It is crucial to examine the potential risks of radicalization, terrorism, and the strain on European security systems that may arise from the mass migration. By understanding these security implications, politicians can develop comprehensive strategies to ensure the safety and well-being of both the migrants and the host communities.

The management of the refugee crisis also has significant political and social consequences. It impacts domestic politics, public opinion, and policy-making. Policymakers must consider the implications of their actions on these fronts and strive to find a balance between humanitarian responsibilities and national interests.

Moreover, the Arab migration into Europe has implications for social cohesion and multiculturalism. Potential cultural clashes, tensions, and the need for social integration policies must be addressed to ensure that diverse communities can coexist harmoniously.

The rise of far-right political movements and parties in response to the mass migration is another pressing issue. It is essential to study their platforms, rhetoric, and impact on European politics to effectively counteract any divisive and discriminatory ideologies.

Furthermore, the political and social consequences of the international community's response to the migration crisis must be analyzed. This includes examining the role of international organizations, cooperation between European countries, and the impact on foreign relations.

The strain on healthcare and welfare systems in European countries due to the influx of Arab migrants also needs to be investigated. This analysis should focus on healthcare access, social services, and public expenditure implications to ensure the provision of adequate support to both the migrants and the host communities.

Additionally, the challenges and opportunities related to the integration of Arab migrant youth into European education systems must be explored. Educational policies, language support, and the impact on social mobility should be considered to provide the necessary tools for the successful integration of the younger generation.

Lastly, the media representation and public perception of the mass migration of Arabs into Europe should be critically examined. Understanding the role of the media in shaping public perception, stereotypes, and understanding of the issue is crucial to counteract misinformation and promote a more balanced and informed narrative.

By addressing these topics, politicians can gain a comprehensive understanding of the political and social consequences of the Arab migration into Europe. This knowledge will enable them to develop well-informed policies and strategies that foster inclusivity, social cohesion, and economic growth while addressing the challenges and seizing the opportunities presented by this significant demographic shift.

Impact on European politics and policies

The recent mass migration of Arabs into Europe has had a profound impact on European politics and policies. This section explores the various dimensions of this impact, shedding light on the potential political and social consequences of the influx of Arab migrants. It also delves into the economic, integration, security, refugee crisis management, social cohesion, political polarization, humanitarian response, healthcare, education, and media representation aspects associated with this migration.

Firstly, the economic consequences of the mass migration are examined, including the effects on local job markets, wages, and economic growth. Policymakers need to understand how the arrival of Arab migrants influences labor markets, both positively and negatively, and how it can impact economic growth in the long run.

Secondly, the challenges faced by Arab migrants in terms of social and cultural integration are explored. Language barriers, discrimination, and the formation of identity are crucial factors that need to be addressed to ensure the successful integration of Arab migrants into European societies.

The potential security implications of the mass migration are also analyzed. Policymakers must carefully consider the risk of radicalization, terrorism, and the strain on European security systems that can arise from the migration of Arab individuals.

Additionally, the political and social consequences of how European countries are managing the refugee crisis are discussed. This includes examining the impact on domestic politics, public opinion, and policy-making processes. The section also delves into the effects of the migration on social cohesion and multiculturalism in European societies, including potential cultural clashes and tensions.

The rise of far-right political movements and parties in response to the mass migration is studied, analyzing their platforms, rhetoric, and impact on European politics. Understanding the reasons behind the rise of such movements is crucial for policymakers seeking to address this issue effectively.

The political and social consequences of the international community's response to the migration crisis are also analyzed. This includes the role of international organizations, cooperation between European countries, and the impact on foreign relations.

Furthermore, the strain on healthcare and welfare systems in European countries due to the influx of Arab migrants is investigated. Policymakers need to understand the implications for healthcare access, social services, and public expenditure.

The challenges and opportunities related to the integration of Arab migrant youth into European education systems are also explored. Educational policies and language support play a vital role in facilitating the social mobility of these young individuals.

Lastly, the role of media in shaping public perception, stereotypes, and understanding of the mass migration issue is examined. Policymakers must be aware of how the media portrays the arrival of Arab migrants and its potential impact on public opinion.

In conclusion, the mass migration of Arabs into Europe has significant implications for European politics and policies. This section provides a comprehensive overview of the various dimensions of this impact, equipping politicians with the knowledge and insights needed to effectively address the political and social consequences associated with the influx of Arab migrants.

Countering far-right movements: strategies and challenges

In recent years, Europe has experienced a significant influx of Arab migrants, resulting in potential political and social consequences that have prompted the need for effective strategies to counter the rise of far-right movements. This section explores the strategies and challenges associated with countering these movements and aims to provide politicians with valuable insights into addressing this pressing issue.

One of the key challenges in countering far-right movements is understanding the underlying factors that contribute to their rise. Economic impact plays a crucial role, as the mass migration of Arabs into Europe has the potential to impact local job markets, wages, and economic growth. Policymakers must develop comprehensive economic strategies to alleviate concerns and minimize the negative effects on the economy.

Integration challenges are another significant aspect to consider. Arab migrants face various obstacles in terms of social and cultural integration, such as language barriers, discrimination, and identity formation. Politicians should prioritize the implementation of inclusive policies that address these challenges and promote social cohesion.

Security concerns cannot be overlooked, as the mass migration may pose potential risks in terms of radicalization, terrorism, and the strain on European security systems. Policymakers must work closely with security agencies to develop effective strategies for monitoring and addressing these security threats.

Refugee crisis management is a critical issue that demands political attention. European countries' management of the refugee crisis has political and social consequences, impacting domestic politics, public opinion, and policy-making. Politicians should prioritize humanitarian responses, ensuring efficient and fair distribution of resources and fostering international cooperation.

The mass migration of Arabs into Europe also has implications for social cohesion and multiculturalism. Cultural clashes and tensions may arise, necessitating the development of social integration policies that promote understanding, tolerance, and respect among different communities.

The rise of far-right political movements in response to the migration crisis must be carefully studied. Analyzing their platforms, rhetoric, and impact on European politics is crucial for countering their influence effectively.

International cooperation and humanitarian response are essential in managing the migration crisis. The political and social consequences of the international community's response, including the role of international organizations and cooperation between European countries, should be thoroughly examined.

The strain on healthcare and welfare systems is another challenge that needs to be addressed. Policymakers should assess the implications for healthcare access, social services, and public expenditure to ensure the sustainability of these systems.

Education and youth integration are key components in fostering successful integration. Policies that support the integration of Arab migrant youth into European education systems, including language support and promoting social mobility, are essential for their future prospects.

Lastly, media representation and public perception play a significant role in shaping the narrative around the mass migration of Arabs into Europe. Policymakers should critically analyze the role of the media in shaping public perception, addressing stereotypes, and promoting a more nuanced understanding of the issue.

In conclusion, countering far-right movements in response to the mass migration of Arabs into Europe requires a comprehensive and multi-faceted approach. By addressing economic, integration, security, and social challenges, policymakers can work towards fostering a more inclusive and cohesive European society. International cooperation, humanitarian response, and responsible media representation are crucial in effectively countering the rise of far-right movements and ensuring a brighter future for all.

Section 8: Humanitarian response and international cooperation: analyzing the political and social consequences of the international community's response to the migration crisis, including the role of international organizations, cooperation between European countries, and the impact on foreign relations.

Role of international organizations: UN, EU, etc.

The mass migration of Arabs into Europe has presented a significant political and social wake-up call for politicians around the world. In this section, we will explore the role of international organizations such as the United Nations (UN) and the European Union (EU) in addressing the various challenges and consequences associated with this migration crisis.

The UN, as a global organization committed to maintaining international peace and security, has played a crucial role in coordinating efforts to manage the refugee crisis. Through its various agencies, such as the United Nations High Commissioner for Refugees (UNHCR), the UN has been actively involved in providing humanitarian assistance and protection to Arab migrants in Europe. The UNHCR has been instrumental in identifying and registering refugees, ensuring their access to basic necessities, and advocating for their rights and well-being.

Similarly, the EU has taken a collaborative approach in addressing the migration crisis. The EU's common asylum policy aims to provide a unified response to the influx of migrants, ensuring a fair and efficient system for processing asylum claims. The European Commission has also provided financial support to member states facing significant migration pressures, assisting in the establishment of reception centers and the integration of migrants into European societies.

The role of international organizations goes beyond immediate crisis management. They also play a vital role in promoting long-term solutions and cooperation between countries. The UN and the EU have facilitated dialogue and coordination between member states, encouraging the sharing of best practices, and fostering a collective approach to addressing the challenges posed by the mass migration of Arabs into Europe.

Furthermore, international organizations have been instrumental in raising awareness and advocating for the rights of Arab migrants. They have played a crucial role in shaping public opinion and challenging negative stereotypes through campaigns and initiatives aimed at promoting understanding and empathy.

In conclusion, the role of international organizations such as the UN and the EU in addressing the political and social consequences of the mass migration of Arabs into Europe cannot be overstated. Their efforts in providing humanitarian assistance, coordinating responses, and promoting long-term solutions are crucial for ensuring the well-being and integration of Arab migrants into European societies. As politicians, it is imperative to recognize and support the role of these organizations in managing the refugee crisis effectively.

Cooperation between European countries: burden-sharing and solidarity

In the wake of the recent mass migration of Arabs into Europe, the issue of burden-sharing and solidarity among European countries has become a pressing concern. As politicians, it is crucial for us to address this issue and find effective solutions that can alleviate the challenges posed by the influx of migrants.

The mass migration of Arabs into Europe has had significant political and social consequences. It has tested the limits of our societies, exposing the vulnerabilities of our integration processes and highlighting the need for a coordinated approach. This section will delve into the importance of cooperation between European countries in addressing the challenges associated with the migration crisis.

Burden-sharing is a key aspect of managing the refugee crisis. It involves the fair distribution of responsibilities and resources among European countries. By sharing the burden, we can ensure that no single country is overwhelmed by the influx of migrants. This requires a comprehensive and coordinated response that includes financial and logistical support, as well as the establishment of effective mechanisms for relocation and resettlement.

Solidarity is equally important in this context. It entails a sense of shared responsibility and a commitment to supporting one another in times of crisis. Solidarity should extend beyond financial and logistical assistance. It should also manifest in a willingness to address the root causes of migration, such as conflicts, poverty, and lack of opportunities, through diplomatic efforts and development aid.

Cooperation between European countries is crucial for the success of burden-sharing and solidarity initiatives. It requires effective communication, coordination, and collaboration among policymakers, government agencies, and civil society organizations. Sharing best practices and lessons learned can also contribute to the development of more efficient and sustainable solutions.

Furthermore, cooperation can also help in mitigating the security implications of the mass migration. By sharing intelligence, enhancing border control measures, and collaborating on counter-terrorism efforts, European countries can work together to ensure the safety and security of their citizens.

In conclusion, the cooperation between European countries is paramount in addressing the challenges posed by the mass migration of Arabs into Europe. Burden-sharing and solidarity are essential components of an effective response to the refugee crisis. By working together, we can not only manage the immediate consequences but also foster long-term solutions that promote social cohesion, economic growth, and security. Only through cooperation can we ensure a sustainable and inclusive future for both the migrants and our societies.

Impact on foreign relations: regional and global dynamics

The mass migration of Arabs into Europe has had significant implications for regional and global dynamics, impacting foreign relations in various ways. This section examines the political and social consequences of this migration on a global scale, addressing the concerns and challenges faced by politicians in navigating these dynamics.

One of the key aspects to consider is the effect on regional stability. The influx of Arab migrants has the potential to strain relations between European countries and their neighboring regions, particularly in the Middle East. This could be due to issues such as the perception of Europe as a destination for migrants, the strain on resources and infrastructure in host countries, and the geopolitical implications of such a large-scale migration.

Furthermore, the migration crisis has highlighted the need for international cooperation. European countries have been grappling with the challenge of managing the refugee crisis, and this has necessitated collaboration with countries outside of Europe. The response of international organizations, such as the United Nations and the

European Union, has also played a crucial role in shaping foreign relations and cooperation.

The migration crisis has also had implications for global security. Concerns about potential radicalization and terrorism have been raised, with politicians being tasked with addressing these security risks. The strain on European security systems has necessitated increased cooperation and intelligence sharing among European countries, as well as with countries of origin and transit.

Another important aspect to consider is the impact on public opinion and domestic politics. The refugee crisis has fueled political polarization and the rise of far-right movements in many European countries. Politicians must grapple with the consequences of these movements, including their impact on policies, rhetoric, and overall political landscape.

Additionally, the migration crisis has tested the social cohesion and multiculturalism of European societies. Politicians are faced with the challenge of fostering social integration and addressing cultural clashes and tensions. The formulation of social integration policies becomes crucial in ensuring the successful integration of Arab migrants into European societies.

Lastly, the media plays a significant role in shaping public perception and understanding of the migration crisis. Politicians must navigate the portrayal of the mass migration of Arabs into Europe and address any stereotypes or misconceptions that arise. This is vital in ensuring informed public discourse and avoiding the perpetuation of harmful narratives.

Overall, the mass migration of Arabs into Europe has far-reaching implications for foreign relations, both regionally and globally. Politicians must grapple with the challenges posed by this migration crisis and work towards fostering cooperation, addressing security concerns, promoting social integration, and shaping public perception in a responsible manner.

Lessons from international cooperation: future strategies

In the wake of the recent mass migration of Arabs into Europe, it is imperative for politicians to understand the potential political and social consequences that this phenomenon may entail. In order to effectively address these challenges, it is crucial to explore future strategies based on lessons from international cooperation.

Firstly, the economic impact of the mass migration must be carefully examined. Studies should delve into the effects on local job markets, wages, and economic growth. By understanding these dynamics, policymakers can devise strategies to mitigate any negative repercussions and harness the potential economic benefits that may arise.

Furthermore, integration challenges faced by Arab migrants in European societies must be addressed. Language barriers, discrimination, and identity formation are some of the key obstacles that need to be tackled. Policymakers should focus on creating inclusive policies that promote social and cultural integration, fostering a sense of belonging and cohesion within European societies.

Security concerns should also be thoroughly analyzed. It is vital to assess the potential risks of radicalization, terrorism, and the strain on European security systems resulting from the mass migration. Cooperation between European countries and international organizations is essential in developing comprehensive security strategies to ensure the safety and well-being of both migrants and host communities.

Refugee crisis management requires close scrutiny to understand its political and social consequences. The impact on domestic politics, public opinion, and policy-making should be assessed to formulate effective measures that address the concerns of all stakeholders involved.

The mass migration of Arabs into Europe has the potential to affect social cohesion and multiculturalism. Policymakers should anticipate possible cultural clashes and tensions, and implement social integration policies that promote understanding and harmony among diverse communities.

The rise of far-right political movements and parties in response to the mass migration must be studied. By examining their platforms, rhetoric, and impact on European politics, policymakers can devise strategies to counteract their divisive ideologies and promote inclusive governance.

Humanitarian response and international cooperation play a crucial role in addressing the migration crisis. The political and social consequences of the international community's response, including the role of international organizations and cooperation between European countries, should be carefully analyzed to foster effective collaboration and ensure a coordinated approach.

The strain on healthcare and welfare systems due to the influx of Arab migrants should not be overlooked. Policymakers must investigate the implications for healthcare access, social services, and public expenditure to develop sustainable strategies that uphold the welfare of both migrants and host communities.

Education and youth integration are key areas that require attention. Policies should be developed to address the challenges and opportunities related to the integration of Arab migrant youth into European education systems. Language support and social mobility initiatives should be prioritized to ensure their successful integration and future prospects.

Finally, media representation and public perception of the mass migration should be critically examined. The role of media in shaping public perception, stereotypes, and understanding of the issue should be analyzed to promote accurate and empathetic narratives that foster understanding and solidarity.

By drawing lessons from international cooperation, policymakers can develop future strategies that address the challenges of the Arab migration into Europe. Through comprehensive analysis and collaboration, Europe can navigate this complex issue and create inclusive societies that foster integration and shared prosperity.

Section 9: Healthcare and welfare systems: investigating the strain on healthcare and welfare systems in European countries due to the influx of Arab migrants, analyzing the implications for healthcare access, social services, and public expenditure.

Healthcare access and challenges

The mass migration of Arabs into Europe has presented numerous challenges, particularly in the realm of healthcare access. As politicians, it is crucial to understand the impact this influx has had on healthcare systems and the implications for both Arab migrants and host societies.

One of the primary challenges is the strain placed on healthcare systems. European countries have had to confront the increased demand for medical services, which has often exceeded the capacity of their existing systems. This strain has resulted in longer wait times, overcrowded hospitals, and limited access to specialized care for both Arab migrants and local populations.

Furthermore, language barriers have posed significant challenges in accessing healthcare services. Arab migrants often face communication difficulties, as they may not be proficient in the local language. This language barrier not only hinders effective communication between healthcare providers and patients but also limits the ability of migrants to navigate the healthcare system and understand their rights and entitlements.

Discrimination also exists within healthcare systems, as some Arab migrants may encounter prejudice or bias from healthcare professionals. This discrimination can lead to a lack of trust in healthcare providers and deter individuals from seeking necessary medical attention. Addressing these biases and promoting cultural sensitivity within healthcare settings is essential to ensure equitable access to healthcare for all.

Moreover, the strain on healthcare and welfare systems has financial implications. The increased demand for healthcare services has resulted in higher public expenditure, putting pressure on already stretched budgets. Policymakers must prioritize adequate funding for healthcare and welfare systems to ensure that both Arab migrants and the host population have access to quality care.

Efforts should also be made to improve health literacy among Arab migrants. Providing information on available healthcare services, rights, and entitlements in multiple languages can empower individuals to navigate the system and make informed decisions about their health.

Additionally, it is crucial to recognize the unique healthcare needs of Arab migrant populations. Many migrants have experienced trauma, both during their journey and in their countries of origin. Mental health services should be made accessible and culturally sensitive to address the psychological well-being of Arab migrants.

In conclusion, the mass migration of Arabs into Europe has placed significant strain on healthcare systems. Language barriers, discrimination, and the financial demands have presented challenges in ensuring equitable access to healthcare. As politicians, it is imperative to develop policies that address these challenges, promote cultural sensitivity within healthcare settings, and allocate adequate resources to meet the healthcare needs of both Arab migrants and local populations.

Social services and welfare provision

The recent mass migration of Arabs into Europe has raised significant concerns for politicians regarding the provision of social services and welfare to these new arrivals. The influx of migrants has put a strain on existing social welfare systems, as European countries grapple with the challenge of meeting the needs of a growing population.

One of the key issues that policymakers must address is the impact of the mass migration on healthcare systems. The sudden increase in population has placed a burden on healthcare resources, leading to longer waiting times and stretched services. Politicians must consider how to ensure access to healthcare for both the migrants and the local population, while also managing the cost implications of providing care to a larger number of individuals.

Similarly, the strain on welfare systems cannot be ignored. The influx of migrants has created a need for additional social services, including housing, employment support, and language assistance. Policymakers must devise strategies to meet these needs while also ensuring that the welfare system remains sustainable and does not become overwhelmed.

Education is another area that requires attention. Arab migrant youth face unique challenges when it comes to integrating into European education systems. Language barriers, cultural differences, and a lack of appropriate support can hinder their ability to succeed academically and socially. Politicians must invest in educational policies that address these challenges and provide pathways for social mobility for these young individuals.

Furthermore, the provision of social services must be sensitive to the cultural and religious backgrounds of the Arab migrants. This includes recognizing the importance of cultural diversity and promoting social integration without erasing or marginalizing their identities. Policymakers must work towards creating inclusive policies that foster social cohesion and multiculturalism, while also addressing the potential for cultural clashes and tensions.

Public perception and media representation play a crucial role in shaping attitudes towards the mass migration of Arabs into Europe. Politicians must be aware of the impact that media portrayal can have on public opinion and work towards countering negative stereotypes and promoting a more nuanced understanding of the issue. By engaging with the media and promoting accurate and balanced reporting, policymakers can influence public perception and create an environment of empathy and understanding.

In conclusion, the mass migration of Arabs into Europe has significant implications for social services and welfare provision. Policymakers must address the strain on healthcare and welfare systems, invest in education and youth integration, promote social cohesion and multiculturalism, and shape public perception through responsible media representation. By proactively addressing these issues, politicians can ensure that the potential political and social consequences of the mass migration are managed effectively and in a way that benefits both the migrants and the receiving societies.

Public expenditure and budgetary impact

One of the key concerns surrounding the mass migration of Arabs into Europe is the potential impact on public expenditure and budgets. The influx of migrants places a significant strain on the resources of European countries, including healthcare, welfare, education, and social services. As a result, policymakers and politicians must grapple with the challenge of managing these increased costs while ensuring the well-being and integration of Arab migrants.

The economic consequences of the mass migration are a crucial aspect to consider. The arrival of a large number of migrants can have both positive and negative effects on the local job markets, wages, and overall economic growth. On one hand, migrants can contribute to the labor force and fill gaps in sectors facing labor shortages. On the other hand, increased competition for jobs can lead to lower wages and job insecurity for both migrants and locals.

Furthermore, the strain on healthcare and welfare systems cannot be ignored. European countries must allocate additional resources to ensure that migrants have access to necessary healthcare services and social support. This places a burden on already-stretched budgets and may lead to increased public expenditure in these sectors.

Education is another area affected by the mass migration. European countries need to invest in language support programs and educational policies to facilitate the integration of Arab migrant youth into the education system. This requires additional funding and resources, which can impact public expenditure.

The strain on public expenditure and budgets also has implications for social cohesion and multiculturalism. If resources are not allocated effectively, tensions can arise between different social groups and cultural clashes may occur. It becomes crucial for policymakers to invest in social integration policies and programs to promote understanding and cohesion among different communities.

In order to effectively manage the refugee crisis, European countries must work together and cooperate on various levels. This may require increased international cooperation and coordination, which can also impact public expenditure.

Overall, the mass migration of Arabs into Europe poses significant challenges to public expenditure and budgets. Policymakers and politicians need to carefully consider the economic, social, and cultural implications of the migration in order to allocate resources effectively and ensure the successful integration of Arab migrants into European societies.

Addressing healthcare and welfare challenges

The mass migration of Arabs into Europe has presented numerous political and social consequences that require urgent attention from policymakers. One of the crucial areas that demand immediate focus is addressing the healthcare and welfare challenges posed by this influx of migrants.

The strain on healthcare systems in European countries due to the arrival of Arab migrants cannot be ignored. The sudden increase in population has put significant pressure on already burdened healthcare facilities and resources. The sheer number of migrants has overwhelmed the capacity of existing healthcare systems, leading to longer waiting times, reduced access to healthcare services, and compromised quality of care for both migrants and local populations.

Furthermore, the welfare systems in European countries are also facing immense pressures. The need to provide social services, financial assistance, and housing to a large number of migrants has strained the resources available for the local population. This has resulted in increased public expenditure, leaving policymakers grappling with the challenge of ensuring the sustainability of welfare programs in the face of such overwhelming demands.

The implications of this strain on healthcare and welfare systems are far-reaching. Limited access to healthcare services not only affects the well-being of migrants but also poses public health risks for the wider population. Delayed or inadequate healthcare can lead to the spread of infectious diseases and the exacerbation of existing health conditions, creating a public health crisis that cannot be ignored.

Moreover, the strain on welfare systems can foster social inequality and resentment among the local population. As resources are diverted to cater to the needs of migrants, the provision of social services to vulnerable groups within the domestic population may be compromised. This can lead to social tensions, exacerbating existing divisions and hindering social cohesion.

Addressing the healthcare and welfare challenges requires a comprehensive and coordinated approach. Policymakers need to allocate adequate resources to healthcare systems to ensure timely and quality healthcare services for both migrants and locals. Additionally, efforts should be made to enhance the capacity of welfare systems to meet the demands of a diverse population, while also ensuring that the needs of vulnerable groups within the domestic population are not neglected.

Collaboration between European countries and international organizations is also crucial in managing these challenges. Sharing best practices, exchanging resources, and coordinating efforts can help alleviate the strain on healthcare and welfare systems, ensuring a more equitable distribution of services and resources.

Ultimately, addressing the healthcare and welfare challenges posed by the mass migration of Arabs into Europe is not just a moral imperative but also a necessary step for the overall well-being and social cohesion of European societies. It requires proactive policies, adequate resources, and international cooperation to ensure that healthcare access, social services, and public expenditure are effectively managed in the face of this unprecedented migration crisis.

Section 10: Education and youth integration: exploring the challenges and opportunities related to the integration of Arab migrant youth into

European education systems, examining educational policies, language support, and the impact on social mobility.

Educational policies and inclusivity

In the wake of the recent mass migration of Arabs into Europe, it is crucial for policymakers to address the educational policies and inclusivity measures needed to ensure the successful integration of Arab migrant youth into European societies. This section aims to shed light on the challenges and opportunities related to the education and youth integration aspect of the migration crisis.

Language barriers pose a significant challenge to the educational attainment of Arab migrant youth. In order to facilitate their integration, European countries should prioritize language support programs, including language courses and bilingual education, to enable these students to effectively participate in the education system. Additionally, efforts should be made to enhance the cultural competency of teachers and school staff, providing them with the necessary tools and resources to accommodate the diverse cultural backgrounds of Arab migrant students.

Furthermore, it is essential to recognize the potential social and cultural integration challenges faced by Arab migrant youth. Discrimination and prejudice can have a detrimental impact on their educational experience and overall well-being. To counter this, schools should adopt inclusive policies and create safe and welcoming environments that promote multiculturalism and respect for diversity. This can be achieved through the implementation of anti-bullying campaigns, intercultural exchange programs, and the inclusion of diverse cultural perspectives in the curriculum.

The integration of Arab migrant youth into European education systems also presents an opportunity for social mobility. By equipping these students with the necessary skills and knowledge, European countries can tap into the potential talent and diversity they bring. This requires not only providing quality education but also ensuring equal access and opportunities for all.

Moreover, media representation plays a crucial role in shaping public perception and understanding of the mass migration of Arabs into Europe. The media should strive to provide accurate and unbiased coverage, avoiding the perpetuation of stereotypes and misinformation. This can contribute to fostering a more inclusive and empathetic society, where the educational needs of Arab migrant youth are recognized and addressed.

In conclusion, educational policies and inclusivity are vital aspects of managing the mass migration of Arabs into Europe. By prioritizing language support, promoting cultural inclusivity, and providing equal access to education, European countries can empower Arab migrant youth to thrive academically and socially. This not only benefits the individual students but also contributes to the overall social cohesion and multiculturalism of European societies. It is imperative for policymakers to recognize the importance of investing in the education and integration of Arab migrant youth, as they hold the potential to contribute positively to their new societies and foster a more inclusive and prosperous Europe.

Language support and language acquisition

In the wake of the recent mass migration of Arabs into Europe, one of the key challenges faced by Arab migrants is language barriers. The ability to effectively communicate and understand the language of their host country is crucial for successful integration and social cohesion. Language support programs and initiatives play a vital role in facilitating language acquisition and helping Arab migrants navigate their new surroundings.

Language support programs can take various forms, including language courses, language exchange programs, and cultural integration workshops. These programs not only provide essential language skills but also offer a platform for cultural exchange, fostering understanding and mutual respect between Arab migrants and European societies.

Effective language support is important for several reasons. Firstly, it enables Arab migrants to access employment opportunities. Language skills are vital for securing employment and contributing to the local job market. By providing language support, policymakers can help bridge the gap between the skills and qualifications of Arab migrants and the requirements of the local labor market.

Secondly, language support facilitates social inclusion and integration. By learning the language of their host country, Arab migrants can engage with local communities, establish social networks, and build relationships. This helps combat social isolation and promotes a sense of belonging.

Furthermore, language support programs can help tackle discrimination and promote equal opportunities. By empowering Arab migrants with language skills, they are better equipped to assert their rights, access public services, and challenge discriminatory practices.

Language acquisition also plays a crucial role in identity formation. By learning the language of their new environment, Arab migrants can express their cultural heritage while also embracing their new identity as part of the European society. This process of identity formation is essential for social cohesion and multiculturalism.

To ensure the effectiveness of language support programs, policymakers must allocate sufficient resources and develop comprehensive strategies. This includes providing funding for language courses, promoting intercultural dialogue, and encouraging partnerships between schools, community organizations, and language learning centers.

In conclusion, language support and language acquisition are vital components of successful integration and social cohesion for Arab migrants in Europe. By investing in language support programs, policymakers can empower Arab migrants, enhance their economic prospects, and facilitate their social and cultural integration. Language support is not only a practical necessity but also a powerful tool for promoting equality, understanding, and harmony between Arab migrants and European societies.

Social mobility and educational opportunities

Social mobility and educational opportunities are crucial factors in the successful integration of Arab migrants into European societies. As politicians, it is essential to understand the potential consequences of the mass migration on these aspects and develop effective policies to address the challenges and harness the opportunities.

Education plays a pivotal role in enabling social mobility and providing equal opportunities for all individuals. However, Arab migrant youth face unique challenges in accessing quality education due to language barriers, cultural differences, and discrimination. Language support programs and cultural sensitivity training for educators are necessary to ensure that these students can fully engage in the educational system.

Moreover, educational policies should focus on promoting inclusive classrooms that foster diversity and support the social and emotional well-being of Arab migrant youth. This can be achieved by implementing multicultural curricula, promoting intercultural dialogue, and providing mental health support services.

Investing in the education and skills development of Arab migrant youth not only benefits them individually but also contributes to the economic growth and social cohesion of European societies. By equipping these young individuals with the necessary knowledge and skills, they can actively participate in the job market, contribute to innovation, and become productive members of society.

Furthermore, educational opportunities should extend beyond traditional academic pathways to include vocational training and entrepreneurship programs. By providing diverse educational pathways, Arab migrant youth can explore different career options and pursue fields where their skills and interests align.

It is also crucial to address the negative stereotypes and misperceptions of Arab migrants in the media. Media representation plays a significant role in shaping public perception and can either reinforce stereotypes or promote inclusivity and understanding. Politicians should advocate for responsible media reporting that highlights the contributions and achievements of Arab migrants, encouraging public support for their integration.

In conclusion, social mobility and educational opportunities are vital for the successful integration of Arab migrants into European societies. By addressing the challenges faced by Arab migrant youth in accessing quality education and promoting inclusive educational policies, politicians can create an environment that fosters social cohesion, economic growth, and cultural understanding. Additionally, countering negative media portrayal of Arab migrants is essential to shape public perception and promote a more inclusive and tolerant society.

Promoting youth integration and empowerment

As the mass migration of Arabs into Europe continues to shape political and social landscapes, it is essential for policymakers to address the unique challenges faced by Arab migrant youth. This section aims to explore the importance of promoting youth integration and empowerment in order to foster social cohesion, economic growth, and a more inclusive society.

One of the key challenges faced by Arab migrant youth is the language barrier. Language proficiency is crucial for successful integration into European societies, as it facilitates education, employment, and social interaction. Therefore, policymakers should focus on providing comprehensive language support programs that cater specifically to the needs of young migrants. These programs should not only focus on language acquisition but also on cultural understanding, allowing young migrants to navigate their new environment more effectively.

Discrimination and identity formation are also significant challenges faced by Arab migrant youth. They often experience social exclusion, stereotyping, and prejudice, which can hinder their integration process. Policymakers should implement anti-discrimination measures and promote intercultural dialogue to foster inclusivity and combat xenophobia. Moreover, providing support for the formation of positive identities, rooted in both their Arab heritage and their European identity, will help young migrants develop a strong sense of belonging and contribute positively to their host societies.

Empowering Arab migrant youth economically is another crucial aspect of integration. Policymakers should invest in vocational training programs, entrepreneurship initiatives, and job placement services to enhance the employment prospects of young migrants. By equipping them with the necessary skills and opportunities, policymakers can ensure that they become active contributors to the local job markets and drive economic growth.

Furthermore, policymakers should encourage the active participation of Arab migrant youth in decision-making processes. This can be achieved through the establishment of youth councils, mentorship programs, and leadership development initiatives. By giving them a voice and agency, policymakers can harness the potential of young migrants and empower them to become advocates for their communities.

In conclusion, promoting youth integration and empowerment is crucial for addressing the challenges posed by the mass migration of Arabs into Europe. By prioritizing comprehensive language support, combating discrimination, providing economic opportunities, and fostering youth participation, policymakers can create an inclusive and cohesive society that benefits both host communities and Arab migrant youth alike. It is imperative for politicians to recognize the potential of Arab migrant youth and invest in their integration to ensure a prosperous and harmonious future for Europe.

Section 11: Media representation and public perception: examining how the mass migration of Arabs into Europe is portrayed in the media, analyzing the role of media in shaping public perception, stereotypes, and understanding of the issue.

Media framing and narratives

Media framing and narratives play a crucial role in shaping public perception and understanding of the mass migration of Arabs into Europe. The way the media portrays this issue can have significant political and social consequences, impacting various aspects of European societies.

One key area affected by media framing is the potential political and social consequences of the mass migration. Politicians need to be aware of the implications this influx may have on their respective countries. The media can influence public opinion, which in turn can shape domestic politics and policy-making. By examining media narratives, politicians can better understand how to address the concerns and needs of their constituents.

Another important aspect to consider is the economic impact of the Arab migration. Media framing can influence how the economic consequences of this migration are perceived. It is crucial for politicians to have a clear understanding of the effects on local job markets, wages, and overall economic growth. By studying media narratives, policymakers can make informed decisions on how to manage and mitigate any negative economic effects, while also recognizing the potential benefits that can arise from the influx of new labor.

Integration challenges faced by Arab migrants in European societies are also influenced by media representation. Language barriers, discrimination, and identity formation are all key factors that can affect social and cultural integration. By analyzing media framing, politicians can gain insights into the challenges faced by these migrants and develop effective integration policies that promote social cohesion and multiculturalism.

Security concerns are another critical issue related to the mass migration of Arabs into Europe. Media narratives can shape public perception of the risk of radicalization, terrorism, and strain on European security systems. By examining media framing, politicians can develop strategies to address these concerns, ensuring the safety and well-being of both migrants and host communities.

In addition, media representation plays a crucial role in shaping the humanitarian response and international cooperation in managing the refugee crisis. By understanding how the media portrays the migration crisis, politicians can assess the effectiveness of international organizations and cooperation between European countries. This knowledge can inform policy decisions and help build stronger foreign relations.

Furthermore, media framing can influence public perception of the strain on healthcare and welfare systems due to the influx of Arab migrants. By studying media narratives, politicians can gain insights into the implications for healthcare access, social services, and public expenditure. This understanding can inform policies that ensure the provision of adequate healthcare and welfare support to both migrants and host communities.

Education and youth integration is another area impacted by media representation. By exploring media narratives, politicians can better understand the challenges and opportunities related to the integration of Arab migrant youth into European education systems. This knowledge can inform policies that promote educational opportunities, language support, and social mobility for these young individuals.

Lastly, media representation plays a crucial role in shaping public perception, stereotypes, and understanding of the mass migration of Arabs into Europe. By critically analyzing how the media portrays this issue, politicians can address any misinformation or biases, fostering a more informed and cohesive society.

In conclusion, media framing and narratives have significant implications for politicians and the various niches related to the mass migration of Arabs into Europe. By studying media representation, policymakers can better understand the potential political and social consequences, economic impact, integration challenges, security concerns, refugee crisis management, social cohesion, political polarization, humanitarian response, healthcare and welfare systems, education and youth integration, and public perception of this issue. This knowledge can inform effective policies and strategies that promote the successful integration and well-being of both migrants and host communities.

Stereotypes and biases

In this section, we delve into the pervasive issue of stereotypes and biases surrounding the recent mass migration of Arabs into Europe. As politicians, it is crucial for us to understand and address these stereotypes and biases in order to create inclusive and effective policies that foster social cohesion and integration.

The mass migration of Arabs into Europe has sparked various stereotypes and biases, fueled by misinformation and fear. These stereotypes often portray Arab migrants as a homogeneous group, ignoring the diversity within their communities and failing to recognize their individual stories, skills, and contributions. By perpetuating these stereotypes, we risk overlooking the potential political and social consequences of the migration and hindering the integration process.

One of the main challenges faced by Arab migrants is the language barrier. The inability to communicate effectively can lead to isolation, limited access to employment, and difficulties in social integration. However, it is important to challenge the stereotype that Arab migrants are unwilling to learn the local language. Providing language support programs and investing in language education can help break down these barriers and facilitate integration.

Discrimination against Arab migrants is another significant issue that needs to be addressed. Negative stereotypes perpetuated by media representation and public perception contribute to discriminatory practices in various areas, including employment, housing, and public services. By implementing anti-discrimination policies, promoting diversity in workplaces, and fostering intercultural dialogue, we can combat these biases and create inclusive societies.

Identity formation is also a complex aspect of the integration process for Arab migrants. Navigating between their cultural heritage and the need to adapt to their new surroundings can pose challenges, particularly for the younger generation. Recognizing and celebrating cultural diversity while promoting a shared sense of belonging is crucial for fostering social cohesion and preventing cultural clashes.

Furthermore, it is important to acknowledge the potential security implications of the mass migration. While it is essential to maintain effective security measures, it is equally important to avoid stigmatizing an entire community based on the actions of a few. By promoting dialogue and cooperation between Arab migrants and European security systems, we can create an environment that fosters trust and understanding.

In conclusion, addressing stereotypes and biases surrounding the mass migration of Arabs into Europe is essential for politicians. By challenging these biases, implementing inclusive policies, and promoting intercultural dialogue, we can ensure the successful integration of Arab migrants into European societies. This section serves as a wake-up call, urging politicians to confront these issues head-on and work towards a more inclusive and prosperous future for all.

Media responsibility and ethical reporting

The recent mass migration of Arabs into Europe has brought with it a multitude of political and social consequences that need to be addressed by politicians. As the situation continues to evolve, it is crucial for policymakers to understand the role of media responsibility and ethical reporting in shaping public perception and understanding of this complex issue.

The media plays a significant role in shaping public opinion and influencing the way people perceive the Arab migration crisis. It is important for journalists and media organizations to uphold their responsibility to provide accurate, unbiased, and ethical reporting. This includes fact-checking, verifying sources, and presenting a balanced view of the situation.

Inaccurate or sensationalized reporting can contribute to the spread of misinformation, stereotypes, and xenophobia. It is the duty of the media to present the facts objectively and to avoid perpetuating harmful narratives that can further polarize society.

Furthermore, media organizations should strive to give voice to all perspectives involved in the migration crisis. This means including the voices and experiences of both Arab migrants and European citizens. By doing so, the media can contribute to a more nuanced and comprehensive understanding of the situation.

Media outlets should also be aware of the power they hold in shaping public perception and be mindful of the potential consequences of their reporting. The media has the ability to influence public opinion, which can in turn impact political decisions and policies. It is important for journalists to be aware of this power and to use it responsibly.

Additionally, media organizations should make efforts to counter stereotypes and promote a more accurate understanding of the Arab migration crisis. This can be achieved through responsible reporting that challenges misconceptions, provides context, and highlights the diverse experiences of Arab migrants.

Ultimately, media responsibility and ethical reporting are essential in addressing the political and social consequences of the Arab migration crisis. By providing accurate and balanced coverage, media organizations can contribute to a more informed public debate and help shape policies that are based on a comprehensive understanding of the issue. It is the responsibility of politicians to advocate for media organizations to uphold these ethical standards and ensure that the public receives accurate and unbiased information.

Enhancing accurate representation and public awareness

In the section of "Enhancing accurate representation and public awareness," we delve into the importance of ensuring that the mass migration of Arabs into Europe is accurately represented and that the general public is well-informed about the political and social consequences of this phenomenon. This section aims to address the concerns of politicians regarding the need for accurate information and its impact on decision-making processes.

Public awareness is crucial in shaping public opinion and fostering social cohesion. Therefore, it is imperative to counter misinformation and stereotypes that may arise in media coverage. The media plays a significant role in shaping public perception and understanding of the migration crisis. Therefore, it is crucial to analyze media representation and its influence on the general public's perception of Arab migrants.

To enhance accurate representation, it is essential to engage with various stakeholders, including community leaders, academics, and representatives of Arab migrant communities. By including diverse perspectives, we can foster a more nuanced understanding of the challenges faced by Arab migrants and the potential benefits they bring to European societies.

Furthermore, this section explores the role of education in promoting integration and social mobility for Arab migrant youth. Educational policies, language support, and the provision of equal opportunities are key factors in ensuring the successful integration of Arab migrant youth into European education systems.

In addition to education, healthcare and welfare systems are also significantly impacted by the mass migration of Arabs into Europe. The strain on these systems requires careful analysis to ensure that healthcare access and social services are not compromised. This section investigates the implications for healthcare access, social services, and public expenditure.

To address the concerns of politicians, this section emphasizes the need for evidence-based policy-making. Accurate data and comprehensive research are essential in understanding the economic impact, integration challenges, security concerns, and social cohesion issues resulting from the mass migration of Arabs into Europe. By relying on sound research and analysis, policymakers can make informed decisions that benefit both Arab migrants and European societies.

In conclusion, this section highlights the importance of enhancing accurate representation and public awareness regarding the mass migration of Arabs into Europe. By countering misinformation, engaging with various stakeholders, and relying on evidence-based policy-making, we can navigate the challenges and opportunities presented by this migration crisis. Ultimately, by fostering accurate representation and public awareness, we can build more inclusive and cohesive societies in Europe.

Conclusion: Lessons learned and policy recommendations

Summarizing the key findings and insights from the book

Summarizing the key findings and insights from the book "Arab Migration into Europe: A Political and Social Wake-up Call for Politicians"

In "Arab Migration into Europe: A Political and Social Wake-up Call for Politicians," the author delves into the recent mass migration of Arabs into Europe and its potential political and social consequences. The book explores various niches related to this topic, including the economic impact, integration challenges, security concerns, refugee crisis management, social cohesion and multiculturalism, political polarization and far-right movements, humanitarian response and international cooperation, healthcare and welfare systems, education and youth integration, and media representation and public perception.

One of the key findings of the book is the economic impact of the mass migration of Arabs into Europe. It examines how this influx affects local job markets, wages, and overall economic growth. The book highlights the need for policymakers to address these consequences effectively and develop strategies to ensure a balanced economic outcome.

Another significant insight is the integration challenges faced by Arab migrants in European societies. The book discusses language barriers, discrimination, and identity formation as key obstacles to their social and cultural integration. It emphasizes the importance of implementing comprehensive integration policies to foster a harmonious and inclusive society.

In terms of security concerns, the book analyzes the potential risks of radicalization, terrorism, and the strain on European security systems due to the mass migration. It calls for a robust and coordinated approach to address these security threats and safeguard the safety of both migrants and European citizens.

The book also delves into the political and social consequences of how European countries are managing the refugee crisis. It examines the impact on domestic politics, public opinion, and policy-making. The author emphasizes the need for a humanitarian and cooperative response among European nations to effectively manage the crisis and mitigate its repercussions.

Furthermore, the book explores the effects of the Arab migration on social cohesion and multiculturalism in European societies. It highlights the potential for cultural clashes and tensions and emphasizes the importance of implementing social integration policies to foster understanding and acceptance among different communities.

The rise of far-right political movements and parties in response to the mass migration is another key finding discussed in the book. It analyzes their platforms, rhetoric, and impact on European politics, highlighting the need for inclusive political discourse and policies to counteract their divisive influence.

The book also delves into the political and social consequences of the international community's response to the migration crisis. It analyzes the role of international organizations, cooperation between European countries, and the impact on foreign relations. The author emphasizes the importance of a humanitarian response and effective international cooperation to address the challenges posed by the mass migration.

Additionally, the book investigates the strain on healthcare and welfare systems in European countries due to the influx of Arab migrants. It analyzes the implications for healthcare access, social services, and public expenditure. The author calls for comprehensive policies to ensure the sustainability and accessibility of these systems.

The challenges and opportunities related to the integration of Arab migrant youth into European education systems are also explored in the book. It examines educational policies, language support, and the impact on social mobility. The author emphasizes the importance of inclusive educational practices to empower migrant youth and enhance their prospects for success.

Finally, the book examines how the mass migration of Arabs into Europe is portrayed in the media and analyzes the role of media in shaping public perception, stereotypes, and understanding of the issue. It emphasizes the need for accurate and balanced media representation to promote informed public discourse and combat misinformation and prejudice.

Overall, "Arab Migration into Europe: A Political and Social Wake-up Call for Politicians" provides comprehensive insights into the complex issues surrounding the mass migration of Arabs into Europe. It calls upon politicians to address these challenges effectively and develop inclusive policies that promote social cohesion, economic growth, and security for all.

Policy recommendations for politicians and policymakers to address the political and social consequences of Arab migration into Europe.

Policy recommendations for politicians and policymakers to address the political and social consequences of Arab migration into Europe

Introduction:

The recent mass migration of Arabs into Europe has brought about significant political and social consequences that require urgent attention from politicians and policymakers. This section aims to provide key policy recommendations to effectively address these consequences and ensure the successful integration of Arab migrants into European societies.

1. Economic Impact:

Policymakers should invest in comprehensive research to accurately assess the economic consequences of Arab migration. This includes studying the effects on local job markets, wages, and economic growth. Based on these findings, governments should develop targeted employment programs, vocational training initiatives, and entrepreneurship support to facilitate the integration of Arab migrants into the labor market.

2. Integration Challenges:

To overcome social and cultural integration challenges, policymakers should prioritize language acquisition programs, providing language training and resources to Arab migrants. Additionally, measures should be implemented to combat discrimination and promote diversity in

European societies. This can include anti-discrimination legislation, cultural exchange programs, and initiatives to foster intercultural understanding and acceptance.

3. Security Concerns:

Given the potential security implications of the mass migration, policymakers must enhance security cooperation and intelligence sharing between European countries. Additionally, governments should invest in community policing and social programs aimed at preventing radicalization and promoting social cohesion. It is crucial to strike a balance between security measures and protecting the rights and freedoms of Arab migrants.

4. Refugee Crisis Management:

European countries must adopt a unified approach to manage the refugee crisis effectively. Policymakers should establish fair and efficient asylum procedures, ensuring that the burden is shared equitably among member states. Governments should also invest in social infrastructure and public services to address the impact on domestic politics, public opinion, and policy-making.

5. Social Cohesion and Multiculturalism:

To promote social cohesion and multiculturalism, policymakers should implement integration policies that emphasize mutual respect, cultural understanding, and inclusive citizenship. This includes supporting community organizations, promoting intercultural dialogue, and fostering social integration programs that bring together different communities.

6. Political Polarization and Far-Right Movements:

Policymakers should address the rise of far-right political movements by engaging in open and honest dialogue with their supporters, addressing their concerns, and promoting inclusive policies. Efforts should be made to counter misinformation and stereotypes through comprehensive media campaigns that highlight the positive contributions of Arab migrants to European societies.

7. Humanitarian Response and International Cooperation:

Politicians should advocate for increased international cooperation and burden-sharing in managing the migration crisis. This includes supporting organizations such as the UNHCR and IOM while ensuring that the rights and dignity of Arab migrants are protected. Diplomatic efforts should be made to strengthen relationships with countries of origin and transit to address the root causes of migration.

8. Healthcare and Welfare Systems:

Policymakers should allocate sufficient resources to ensure that healthcare and welfare systems can adequately support Arab migrants and local populations. This includes providing language support and culturally sensitive healthcare services, as well as investing in social welfare programs that promote social cohesion and address social inequalities.

9. Education and Youth Integration:

To facilitate the integration of Arab migrant youth into European education systems, policymakers should provide language support, promote intercultural education, and invest in programs that enhance social mobility. This includes access to quality education, vocational training opportunities, and mentorship programs to help young migrants succeed academically and professionally.

10. Media Representation and Public Perception:

Policymakers should engage with media organizations to promote accurate, balanced, and unbiased reporting on the migration issue. Efforts should be made to challenge stereotypes, dispel misconceptions, and foster a more nuanced understanding of the experiences and contributions of Arab migrants. Governments should also support media literacy programs to equip the public with the skills to critically analyze media representation.

Conclusion:

Addressing the political and social consequences of Arab migration into Europe requires a multi-faceted and comprehensive approach. By implementing these policy recommendations, politicians and policymakers can effectively manage the challenges, promote social cohesion, and ensure the successful integration of Arab migrants into European societies.